I0568759

SWU-800- 007

UNIFORMS OF RUSSIAN ARMY DURING THE YEARS 1825-1855 VOL. 7

UNDER THE REIGN OF NICHOLAS I
EMPEROR OF RUSSIA BETWEEN 1825 TO 1855
GUARDS INFANTRY & GUARD CUIRASSIERS REGIMENTS

From the Viskovatov's greatest work:
"Historical description of the clothing and
arms of the Russian Army"

English translation by Mark Conrad

SOLDIERSHOP PUBLISHING

AUTHOR

Aleksandr Vasilevich Viskovatov born 22 April (4 May New Style) 1804, died 27 February (11 March) 1858 in St. Petersburg, Russian military historian. He graduated from the 1st Cadet Corps and served in the artillery, the hydrographic depot of the Naval Ministry, and then in the Department of Military Educational Institutions. He mainly studied historical artifacts and the histories of military units. Viskovatov's greatest work was the Historical Description of the Clothing and Arms of the Russian Army.

PUBLISHING'S NOTE

None of **unpublished** images or text of our book may be reproduced in any format without the expressed written permission of Soldiershop.com when not indicate as marked with license creative commons 3.0 or 4.0. The publisher remains to disposition of the possible having right for all the doubtful sources images or not identifies. Our trademark: Soldiershop Publishing ©, The names of our series: Soldiers&Weapons, Battlefield, War in colour, PaperSoldiers, Soldiershop e-book etc. are herein © by Soldiershop.com.

NOTE ABOUT BOOK PRINTING BEFORE 1925

This book may contain text or images coming from a reproduction of a book published before 1925 (over seventy years ago). No effort has been made to modernize or standardize the spelling used in the original text, so this book may have occasional imperfections such as missing or blurred pages, poor pictures, errant marks, etc. that were either part of the original artifact, or were introduced by the scanning process. We believe this work is culturally important, and despite the imperfections, have elected to bring it back into print (digital and/or paper) as part of our continuing commitment to the preservation of printed works worldwide. We appreciate your understanding of the imperfections in the preservation process, and hope you enjoy this valuable book. Now this book is purpose re-built and is proof-read and re-type set from the original to provide an outstanding experience of reflowing text, also for an ebook reader. However Soldiershop publishing added, enriched, revised and overhauled the text, images, etc. of the cover and the book. Therefore, the job is now to all intents and purposes a derivative work, and the added, new and original parts of the book are the copyright of Soldiershop. On this second unpublished part of the book none of images or text may be reproduced in any format without the expressed written permission of Soldiershop. Almost many of the images of our books and prints are taken from original first edition prints or books that are no longer in copyright and are therefore public domain. We have been a specialized bookstore for a long time so we (and several friends antiquarian booksellers) have readily available a lot of ancient, historical and illustrated books not in copyright. Each of our prints, art designs or illustrations is either our own creation, or a fully digitally restoration by our computer artists, or non copyrighted images. All of our prints are "tagged" with a registered digital copyright. Soldiershop remains to disposition of the possible having right for all the doubtful sources images or not identifies.

LICENSES COMMONS

Much of the text in this book are from the *"Memoirs of the Empress Catherine II., by Catherine II, Empress of Russia"* This book is for the use of anyone anywhere at no cost and with almost no restrictions whatsoever. You may copy it, give it away or re-use it under the terms of the similar creative commons License. This book may utilize material marked with license creative commons 3.0 or 4.0 (CC BY 4.0), (CC BY-ND 4.0), (CC BY-SA 4.0) or (CC0 1.0). We give appropriate attribution credit and indicate if change were made below in the acknowledgements field.

ACKNOWLEDGEMENTS

A Special Thanks to NYPL and other institutions for their kindly permission to use some images of his archives, collections or books used in our book.

Title: **UNIFORMS OF RUSSIAN ARMY DURING THE YEARS 1825-1855. VOL. 7** -Under the reign of Nicholas I emperor of Russia between 1825-1855

By A.V.Viskovatov. Serie edit by Luca S. Cristini. First edition by Soldiershop. January 2019

Cover & Art Design: Luca S. Cristini. Plates re-colorations by Anna Cristini. ISBN code: 978-88-93274098

Published by Luca Cristini Editore, via Orio 35/4- 24050 Zanica (BG) ITALY. www.soldiershop.com

UNIFORMS OF THE RUSSIAN ARMY DURING THE YEARS 1825-1855 VOL. 7

UNDER THE REIGN OF NICHOLAS I EMPEROUR OF
RUSSIA BETWEEN 1825 AND 1855

*

GUARDS INFANTRY & GUARDS CUIRASSIER REGIMENTS

Portrait of the Emperor Nicholas I 1856 by Vladimir Dmitrievich Sverchkov

HISTORICAL DESCRIPTION OF THE CLOTHING AND ARMS
OF THE RUSSIAN ARMY - A.V. VISKOVATOV
(First English translation by Mark Conrad)

Soldiershop is glad to presents the complete collection of the great job made by A.V. Viskovatov dedicated to the uniforms and weapons belonging from the first Zar and Russian emperors to the Russian army during the Napoleonic period, until 1860 about. The time we considered in this volume corresponds to the reigns of Nicholas I that was the Emperor of Russia from 1825 until 1855. He was also the King of Poland and Grand Duke of Finland. He is best known as a political conservative whose reign was marked by geographical expansion, repression of dissent, economic stagnation, poor administrative policies, a corrupt bureaucracy, and frequent wars that culminated in Russia's defeat in the Crimean War of 1853–56.

Our reprint in based on the original 19th century volumes. This part is distributed at now on six volumes.

Our new edition, the first ever published in English, both on paper and digital format, boasts a large number of color plates, many of them unpublished and re-coloured by our team of expert artists and scholars of uniformology. Each volume is based on 100 color plates or more, always accompanied by the original translated text which describes the subjets of the plates.

A unique work in its genre, a must have in any respecting collection!

Aleksandr Vasilevich Viskovatov born 22 April (4 May New Style) 1804, died 27 February (11 March) 1858 in St. Petersburg, Russian military historian. He graduated from the 1st Cadet Corps and served in the artillery, the hydrographic depot of the Naval Ministry, and then in the Department of Military Educational Institutions. He mainly studied historical artifacts and the histories of military units. Viskovatov's greatest work was the Historical Description of the Clothing and Arms of the Russian Army (Vols. 1-30, St. Petersburg, 1841-62; 2nd ed. Vols. 1-34, St. Petersburg - Novosibirsk - Leningrad, 1899-1948). This work is based on a great quantity of archival documents and contains four thousand colored illustrations.

Viskovatov was the author of Chronicles of the Russian Army (Books 1-20, St. Petersburg, 1834-42) and Chronicles of the Russian Imperial Army (Parts 1-7, St. Petersburg, 1852). He collected valuable material on the history of the Russian navy which went into A Short Overview of Russian Naval Campaigns and General Voyages to the End of the XVII Century (St. Petersburg, 1864; 2nd edition Moscow, 1946). Together with A.I. Mikhailovskii-Danilevskii he helped prepare and create the Military Gallery in the Winter Palace. He wrote the historical military inscriptions for the walls of the Hall of St. George in the Great Palace of the Kremlin. (From the article in the Soviet Military Encyclopedia.)

CONTENTS

*

Preface pag. 5

HISTORICAL DESCRIPTION OF THE CLOTHING AND ARMS OF THE RUSSIAN ARMY

Guards Infantry and Guards Cuirassier Regiments 1825-1855

CHANGES IN THE UNIFORMS AND EQUIPMENT OF TEMPORARY FORCES FROM 1801 TO 1825.

24 – GUARDS HEAVY INFANTRY [GVARDEISKAYA TYAZHELAYA PEKHOTA].

25 December 1825 - In the Life-Guards Preobrazhenskii and Semenovskii Regiments, officers and lower ranks who on 19 November of this year were in companies bearing the name of EMPEROR ALEXANDER I, now resting in God, are ordered to have on their **epaulettes** and **shoulder straps** the **monogram** of HIS MAJESTY, under a crown, in silver for officers and in brass for lower ranks (Illus. 607) [1].

11 February 1826 - Officers in Guards heavy infantry regiments (Preobrazhenskii, Semenovskii, Izmailovskii, Moscow, Grenadier, Pavlovsk, and Lithuania), in place of their previous white pants with high boots, and lower combatant ranks in place of the same white pants but with knee gaiters [kragi], are ordered to have long dark-green **pants** [pantalony] of the pattern introduced at this time for the army infantry, with piping on the side seams: Preobrazhenskii (Illus. 608), Semenovskii, Izmailovskii, Moscow (Illus. 609), Grenadier, and Pavlovsk regiments—red, and in the Lithuania Regiment (Illus. 610)—yellow. Lower ranks at all times, but company-grade officers when in formation and whenever wearing the sash, are to wear black cloth **half-gaiters** [polushiblety] under these pants and over the boots, fastened with five or six small metal buttons the same color as those on the coat. Generals (when in regimental uniform), field-grade officers, and adjutants, while wearing the same pants as for company-grade officers with the troops, are ordered not to have boots with the spurs driven in, and not to wear gaiters. Along with these changes, the horizontal **belt for the knapsack** is to be above the lower buttons on the front of the coat, while the **greatcoat** is carried on the knapsack rolled into a tube in its special oilskin case made of raven's-duck. Clerks and all noncombatant lower ranks in general who have frock coats [syurtuki] are ordered to wear grey riding trousers [reituzy] without stripes [2].

10 May 1826 - Generals, field-grade officers, and adjutants, during the summer, when in formation and obliged to be mounted, are ordered to wear **white linen pants** without integral spats, of the same pattern as the dark-green pants described above (Illus. 611). Also, they are permitted to have suede pants in place of the linen pants, of the same pattern [3].

15 September 1826 - Lower ranks who have served out the regulation number of years for retirement without reproach, yet voluntarily remain in service, are ordered to wear a **gold galloon chevron** [nashivka iz zolotago galuna] on the left sleeve above and in addition to the yellow tape chevrons [nashivki iz zheltago basona] prescribed on 29 March 1825 [4].

12 December 1826 - Officers' rapiers [shpagi] are replaced by **half-sabers** [polusabli] of the same pattern as those introduced on 20 August 1830 for army infantry and described above for Grenadier regiments [5].

1 January 1827 - Officers' epaulettes are to have little forged or stamped **stars** [kovannyya zvezdochki] **as rank distinctions**. These are silver in the Preobrazhenskii, Semenovskii, Izmailovskii, Moscow, Grenadier, and Pavlovsk regiments, and gold in the Lithuania Regiment. Ensigns [praporshchiki] have one, Sublieutenants [Podporuchiki] two, Lieutenants [Poruchiki] three, Staff-Captains [Stabs-Kapitany] four, Major Generals [General-Maiory] two, and Lieutenant Generals [General-Leitenanty] three. Colonels [Polkovniki] and full Generals [polnye Generaly] are not prescribed any stars [6].

14 February 1827 - In the Life-Guards Moscow, Grenadier, and Pavlovsk regiments **cuff flaps**, instead of being dark green with red piping, are ordered to be red without piping (Illus. 612 and 613) [7].

1 March 1827 - The **monogram of EMPEROR ALEXANDER I**, as established on 15 December 1825 for officers and lower ranks of the Life-Guards Preobrazhenskii and Semenovskii regiments, are, in the case of one or the other being released from service, or upon the promotion of the latter to officer rank, to be worn on the breast, on the left side, in a laurel wreath; gilt for officers and bronze for lower ranks (Illus. 614) [8].

31 July 1827 - Numbers and letters on **shako** and **cartridge-pouch covers**, instead of being of yellow cloth, are ordered to be painted on with yellow oil paint [9].

14 December 1827 - The **chevrons** established on 15 September 1826 for the left sleeves of lower ranks are ordered to be gold or silver, according to the non-commissioned officers' galloon in that regiment in which the man who has served out the regulation number of years for retirement voluntarily remains in service [10].

24 March 1828 - The **coats** of lower ranks are not to be tailored with cinches [*peretyazhki*] [11].

24 April 1828 - The following changes were made in articles of uniform and accouterments:

1.) A new model **shako** [*kiver*]: 5 1/2 vershoks [9 5/8 inches] high with a top diameter not less than 5 5/8 vershoks [9 7/8 inches] and not more than 6 vershoks [10 1/2 inches]. The lower diameter is according to the size of the head. The thickness of the upper, lacquered edge is 5/16 vershok [1/2 inch] (Illus. 615, 616, 617, and 618).

2.) With the increase in the shako's height, the **shako plate** [*gerb*] will be of a new, slightly altered form: in the Preobrazhenskii, Semenovskii, Izmailoskii, Moscoe, and Grenadier regiments—with an image of St. George the Bearer of Victory (Illus. 619), and in the Lithuania Regiment—with an image of a Lithuanian horseman within an eagle's shield (Illus. 620).

3.) The **shako cords** [*etishket*] are also of a new pattern, consisting of a white cord around the top of the shako and tassels with bows [*banty*] hanging down on the right even with the lower edge of the shako. For privates these last are completely white and for non-commissioned officers white with orange and black.

4.) The **pouch belt** [*perevyaz'*] and **sword-belt** [*portupeya*] are prescribed to be 2 vershoks [3 1/2 inches] wide; the **shoulder belts for the knapsack** [*rantsevye plechevye remni*] — 1 1/2 vershoks [2 5/8 inches]; and the **belt across the chest** [*nagrudnyi remen*] — 1 1/8 vershoks [2 inches].

5.) **Knapsacks** are to be of calfskin [*telyachaya kozha*] as before but with black leather trim (Illus. 618). The knapsack is prescribed to be 9 vershoks [15 3/4 inches]broad, 8 vershoks [14 inches] high, and 2 1/2 vershoks [4 3/8 inches] wide. The length of the cover from the upper edge is 6 vershoks [10 1/2]inches.

6.) In place of their grey coats [*mundiry*], all **non-combatant non-commissioned officers** are issued dark-green **frock coats** [*syurtuki*] with a single row of buttons and the same collar, cuffs, and shoulder straps as for combatant personnel. **Pants**, however, are grey with red piping on the side seams (Illus. 618).

7.) **Non-combatant craftsmen** [*masterovye*] of the lower ranks, as well as **medical orderlies** [*lazaretnye sluzhiteli*] are to replace their coats with grey cloth **jackets** [*kurtki*] modeled on the coat, while pants are to be as for the non-combatants above (Illus. 621) [12].

18 May 1829 - Non-commissioned officers who have been recommended by higher command for promotion to officer rank by virtue of years of service are permitted to have **silver sword knots** [*serebryanye temlyaki*] [13].

26 December 1829 - All ranks are ordered to have the **buttons** on their coats, frock coats, and greatcoats made with the raised image of a the two-headed eagle prescribed for the shako plate [14].

9 May 1831 - Yellow cloth in the uniforms of the **Life-Guards Lithuania Regiment** is replaced with red, and in the shield on the shako plate, instead of the image of a Lithuanian horseman there is to be an image of St. George the Bearer of Victory, as in the rest of the Guards heavy infantry regiments (Illus. 622) [15].

6 December 1831 - With the granting of the rights and privileges of the Old Guard [*Staraya Gvardiya*] to the **Life-Guards Grenadier and Pavlovsk regiments**, chevrons on the coats of lower ranks are ordered to be yellow instead of white, with red lines or stripes [*reiki ili poloski*], after the example of the rest of the Guards heavy infantry regiments (Illus. 623). Along with this change, the silver galloon, epaulettes, and shako cords for drum majors of both regiments is replaced by gold, and the dark-green officers' shabracks and pistol holders by red ones: in the Life-Guards Grenadier Regiment—with blue [*svetlosinii*] trim, but in the Life-Guards Pavlovsk Regiment—with white trim [16].

1 January 1832 - Generals who have the diamond-studded gold rapiers [*shpagi*] "*za khrabost*" ["for courage"] are not to use **sword knots** with these swords [17].

29 February 1832 - The **Grenadier regiments** included in the Guards heavy infantry—the Emperor of Austria's (from 28 February 1835 to 28 December 1848—Emperor Francis I's) and the King of Prussia's (since 26 May 1840 King Frederick-William III's)—are prescribed new uniform clothing as follows:

a.) For the Emperor of Austria's Regiment—dark-green coat with blue [*svetlosinii*] collar; red piping on the collar, plastron, cuffs, cuff flaps, turn backs, and lining; dark-green pants with red piping; lower ranks' shoulder straps are as before—yellow with a red monogram; officers' epaulettes and the monogram on it are silver, with a yellow field; white buttons with a small grenade with no number; white shako fittings; shako plate of the army pattern, with a grenade and no number. Along with this the previous gold button hole lace on the collar and cuff flaps of officers' coats are replaced with silver (Illus. No. 624).

b.) For the King of Prussia's Regiment—coat and the rest as for the Emperor of Austria's Regiment, but a dark-green collar with red piping (Illus. No. 624) [18].

8

24 March 1832 - In the **Life-Guards Lithuania Regiment** greatcoat collars are ordered to have button holes of red cloth, with a coat button, after the example of the Life-Guards Moscow Regiment (Illus. 625). On this same date, as a supplement to the uniform changes in the Emperor of Austria's and King of Prussia's regiments of 29 February 1832, it is ordered:

a.) In the **Emperor of Austria's Regiment**—officers' frock coats and greatcoats, and the greatcoats of lower ranks, are to be as for the Life-Guards Grenadier Regiment, but with white buttons as prescribed for other uniform items; forage caps are also to be as for that regiment; officers' shabracks and pistol holders are to be dark green with blue [*svetlosinii*] trim and silver galloon, without a star.

b.) In the **King of Prussia's Regiment**—officers' frock coats and greatcoats, and the greatcoats of lower ranks, are to be as for the Life-Guards Pavlovsk Regiment, but with white buttons as prescribed for other uniform items; forage caps are also to be as for that regiment; officers' shabracks and pistol holders are to be dark green with white trim and silver galloon, without a star. [19].

8 June 1832 - Officers are permitted to wear **moustaches** [20].

3 January 1833 - Cloth **half-gaiters** [*polushtiblety*] are abolished for company-grade officers and lower ranks, as are shako covers, cartridge-pouch covers, and sword knots for non-commissioned officers and lower ranks (Illus. 626). The latter are to be worn only by those non-commissioned officers have received them in silver [21].

20 January 1833 - **Shako covers** are left as before [22].

20 February 1833 - All combatant ranks are given new pattern **summer pants** [*pantalony*] or **breeches** [*bryuki*], without buttons or integral spats [*kozyrki*] (Illus. 627) [23].

25 April 1834 - Lower ranks of the **Emperor of Austria's and King of Prussia's regiments** are ordered to have sewn-on lace or button-hole loops [*nashivki ili petlitsy*] of white tape [*bason*] on their coat collars and cuff flaps (Illus. 628) [24].

26 September 1834 - Lower combatant ranks are directed to wear the **knapsack** on two belts lying crosswise over the chest (Illus. 629) [25].

20 August 1835 - It is ordered that:

1.) Officers wear the **knapsack** using only two shoulder belts without any horizontal strap over the chest (Illus. 630). These belts are to be lacquered.

2.) For lower ranks a **linen case** [*kholshchevyi chekhol*] or pocket [*karman*] for the forage cap is to be put on the outside of the knapsack on the side that lies on the soldier's back. These cases are to be made from the linings of wornout coats.

3.) For drummers the **knapsack** is to have one belt as before, worn over the left shoulder [26].

31 January 1836 - Lower ranks' **greatcoats** [*shineli*] are to have nine buttons instead of ten: six along the front opening, two on the shoulder straps, and one on the flap behind [27].

27 April 1836 - **Pompons** are to be lined with black leather [28].

13 May 1836 - **Girths** [*podprugi*] for officers' saddles are to be dark green with red stripes [29].

21 October 1836 - **Shako plumes** [*kivernye sultany*] are to be 11 vershoks [19 1/4 inches] high from the triangular socket to the top, with an upper circumference of 5 2/3 vershoks [10 inches] and a lower one of 4 vershoks [7 inches]. Its weight is to be not more than 54 zolotniks [8 1/10 ounces] [30].

14 January 1837 - Handles of **entrenching tools** [*shantsovye instrumenty*] are no longer to be painted with oil-based paint, but rather the wood is to be varnished [*pokryvat lakom*], and directives for carrying and fitting these tools are confirmed, as described above in detail for Grenadier regiments [31].

15 July 1837 - Officers are given a new pattern of **sash** [*sharf*] that instead of the previous wide lace has narrow, silver lace with three stripes of light-orange and black silk, and is tied with its entire width between the two lower buttons of the coat, as described above in detail for Grenadier regiments [sic, there are no additional details - M.C.] [32].

17 December 1837 - In order to introduce uniformity to officers' **epaulettes**, their pattern is confirmed with the addition of a fourth, narrow braid [*uzkii vitok*], as described above in detail for Grenadier regiments [sic, there are no additional details - M.C.] [33].

18 January 1838 - In summer, regimental **staff-hornists** [*shtab-gornisty*], when obliged to be mounted in formation, are ordered to wear winter trousers [*bryuki*]. Instead of knapsacks they are to have valises [*chemodany*] of the cavalry pattern and their horses are to be with bridles [*uzdechki*], with a saddle patterned after the one for mounted artillerymen, without a shabrack or saddlecloth [*cheprak ili val'trap*] [34].

4 January 1839 - Generals and field and company-grade officers are not to have any bows or bands [*banty*] on the front of their **pants** or **trousers**. These are to be worn completely smooth in the manner prescribed for lower ranks [35].

16 March 1839 - Lower ranks' **pouch belts** [*perevyazi*] and **sword belts** [*portupei*], which were originally 2 1/8 vershoks [3 7/8 inches] wide and then, since 1828, 2 vershoks [3 1/2 inches] wide, are ordered to be 1 1/2 vershoks [2 5/8 inches] wide with strips 1/8 vershok [1/5 inch] from the edge. **Drummers' crossbelts** [*barabannyya perevyazi*] are as before, 2 1/2 vershoks [4 2/5 inches] wide [36].

16 October 1840 - Lower ranks who have earned the right to discharge on indefinite leave [*bezsrochnyi otpusk*] but who voluntarily remain on active service after serving the regulation number of years are to be given **gold galloon chevrons** [*shevrony ili nashivki, iz zolotago galuna*]for the left sleeve, one for every five years of extra service. On this same basis these same chevrons are prescribed for non-commissioned officers who have declined promotion to officer rank and are receiving two-thirds of an ensign's pay, for serving five or more years after declining such promotion [37].

23 January 1841 - The capes [*bolshie vorotniki*] of officers' **greatcoats** are to be 1 arshin [28 inches] long as measured from the lower edge of the collar [*malyi vorotnik*] [38].

8 April 1843 - There are the following changes:

1.) Officers and lower ranks are given a new model **shako** [*kiver*], 4 3/4 vershoks [8 1/3 inches] high and curving slightly inward toward the bottom. New dimensions are prescribed for shako **plumes**: 9 3/4 vershoks [17 inches] high from the socket to the top, an upper circumference of 5 1/4 vershoks [9 1/4 inches], and a lower circumference of 3 1/2 vershoks [6 1/8 inches] [39].

2.) In order to more easily be distinguished from generals' epaulettes, it is directed that **drum-majors' epaulettes** [*tambur-mazhorskie epolety*] have red silk mixed in the gold braided threads and in the hanging fringe (Illus. 631 and 632) [40].

3.) **Rank distinctions** for lower ranks of Guards regiments in the Guards heavy infantry are established, in the form of trim sewn onto shoulder straps [*nashivki na plechevykh pogonakh*], with the following particulars:

1. For sergeants [*feldfebeli*] — wide gold non-commissioned officers' galloon, sewn in one row across the shoulder strap, close to the button hole .

2. For distinguished officer candidates [*portupei-praporshchiki*] and officer candidates [*podpraporshchiki*] — narrow gold galloon around the edge of the shoulder straps.

3. For section non-commissioned officers [*otdelennye unter-ofitsery*] — narrow wool tape [*sherstyanyi bason*], yellow with red stripes, in three rows across the shoulder strap.

4. For other non-commissioned officers [*prochie unter-ofitsery*] — the same tape, sewn on the same but in two rows.

5. For lance-corporals [*yefreitory*] — the same tape, sewn on the same but in one row.

Both Grenadier regiments of the Guards heavy infantry are prescribed the sewn-on rank distinctions established for Grenadier regiments of the army infantry [41].

10 May 1843 - The covers of **cartridge-pouches** [*patronnyya sumki*] are not to have any break on top [*bez pereloma vverkhu*], and are to measure [with the cover sewn onto the body of the pouch]: length — 5 vershoks [8 3/4 inches], width at the top edge — 5 1/2 vershoks [9 5/8 inches], width at the bottom edge — 6 vershoks [10 1/2 inches] [42].

2 January 1844 - Officers are to have an oblong, metal **cockade** [*kokarda*] on the band of their forage caps, in the same colors as the cockade on officers' hats (Illus. 633) [43].

8 January 1844 - Staff-hornists [*shtab-gornisty*], when mounted in formation, are permitted to have spurs [44].

8 May 1844 - It is directed that shakos [*kivera*] be replaced by **helmets** [*kaski*] of black lacquered leather, with two visors, mountings of the same color as the buttons, a horsehair plume [*sultan*], and the previous shako plate, all of the pattern of the helmets introduced at this time in the army and described above in detail for Grenadier regiments (Illus. 634, 635, 636, 637, and 638) [45].

20 May 1844 - A new scheme for lower ranks' **forage caps** is approved, on the basis of which the piping on the upper edge is to be: in the 1st battalion—red, in the 2nd—white, and in the 3rd—blue [*svetlosinii*]. The cap band colors remain as before, red in the Preobrazhenskii, Moscow, and Lithuania regiments, blue [*svetlosinii*] in the Semenovskii, Grenadier, and Emperor Francis I's regiments, and white with two red lines of piping in the Izmailovskii, Pavlovsk, and King Frederick-William III's Grenadier regiments. Company numbers and Cyrillic letters are cut out as before, on yellow cloth. For officers of all regiments the piping on the top edge of the forage cap is red [46].

17 November 1844 - Instructions for storing and protecting the **helmet plume** [*kasochnyi sultan*] are approved, as set forth in detail above for Grenadier regiments [47].

7 December 1844 - Generals who are wearing a regimental coat [*polkovoi mundir*] when not on duty are to have a **white**

plume [*sultan*] on the hat [*shlyapa*] instead of a black one [48].

4 January 1845 - Officers' helmets are to have, on the right side under the chin-scales, a metal **cockade** patterned after the one worn on the hat [Illus. 639] [49].

9 August 1845 - The **plume** is not to be worn with camp dress [*pre lagernoi forme*], even if those personnel entitled to plumes are wearing coats [*mundiry*] (Illus. 640) [50].

14 April 1846 - Officers of the L.-Gds. Pavlovsk Regiment are allowed to wear helmets with a black plume instead of Grenadier caps in all those situations when they are not in formation, in town uniform [*gorodskaya forma*] (Illus. 641) [51].

26 April 1846 - Instead of a brass spear point, **unit guidons** [*zhalonerskie znaki*, from Fr. *jalonner* — M.C.] are to have a brass ball [52].

23 June 1846 - With the introduction of percussion-lock weapons, a description for fitting the **firing-cap pouch** [*kapsyulnaya sumka*] is approved (see Grenadier regiments) (Illus. 642) [53].

19 May 1847 - Barbers, chaplains' assistants, supply-train personnel, provosts, lazaret orderlies [*lazaretnye sluzhiteli*], and craftsmen are ordered to have **forage caps** of grey cloth, with a black leather visor and similar chinstrap, a cap band also of grey cloth, and red piping around the top of the crown and both edges of the band. Clerks, medics [*fel'dshery*], apothecary apprentices, the nurse [*nadziratel' bol'nykh*], and other lower noncombatant ranks are prescribed dark-green **forage caps** with a black leather visor and chinstrap, and a band and piping as for combatant lower ranks [54].

29 November 1847 - **Distinguished officer candidates** [*portupei-praporshchikam i portupei-yunkeram*] who, based on the regulations concerning the acceptance of young noblemen for service in the Guards, carry out officers' responsibilities in their regiments after passing an examination, are ordered to wear an officer's **half-saber** [*poulsablya*] instead of a short sword [*tesak*] (Illus. 643) [55].

9 January 1848 - On those days when they are obliged to remain in ceremonial dress [*prazdnichnaya forma*] after the mounting of the guard [*posle razvoda*], generals and field and company-grade officers are permitted to wear the **frock coat** with helmet and plume for walking-out (Illus. 644) [56].

19 April 1849 - With the introduction of new **English signal bugles** [*Angliiskie signalnye rozhki*], the means of fitting them to their belts is established, as described in detail for Grenadier regiments [57].

14 September 1849 - Approval is given as to the type of **percussion pistol** [*udarnyi pistolet*] for officers (see Grenadier regiments) [58].

9 and 25 November 1849 - The manner of fitting the **helmet** is confirmed (see Grenadier regiments) [59].

24 December 1849 - The grip on the hilt of the **gold half-saber** awarded for bravery is to be gold instead of wrapped with black lacquered leather [60].

17 January 1851 - Approval is given to a description of the manner of gathering up and folding back the skirts [*poly*] of the **greatcoat** (see Grenadier regiments) (Illus. 645) [61].

8 July 1851 - With the issue to the forces of **percussion weapons** with cases or covers for firing nipples [*sterzhni*], the frizzen cover [*polunagalishche*] used up to now is withdrawn. Additionally, approval is given to patterns and descriptions of the **infantry drum** [*pekhotnyi baraban*], **water flask** [*vodonosnaya flyaga*], **greatcoat strap** [*shinelnyi remen'*], **sword belt** [*portupeya*], **crossbelt** [*perevyaz'*], and **cover for the nipple of percussion weapons** [*chekhol na sterzhen' dlya udarnykh ruzhei*], in agreement in every respect with those conformed on this day for Grenadier regiments and other units of army infantry, with the only differences being that in the guards infantry the body of the drum is prescribed to be of red brass instead of yellow, and the oval of the device on the body is larger, namely: a long axis of 5 1/2 vershoks [9 5/8 inches] and a short one of 4 vershoks [7 inches] [62].

20 October 1851 - Approval is given to the list and description of items that the soldier is to have in his **knapsack** (see Grenadier regiments) [63].

26 January 1852 - Noncombatant lower ranks with **forage caps** of grey cloth are to have a cap band in the color of the collar of the unit to which they belong (Illus. 646) [64].

17 October 1852 - Generals, field and company-grade officers, and adjutants are ordered to have when in formation: for parade uniform a **shabrack** of the previous pattern, and for campaign uniform a *vice-shabrack* [*vitse-cheprak*] of dark-green cloth, for which the following description is confirmed: instead of the colored cloth stripe with two rows of galloon as prescribed for the parade shabrack, the vice-shabrack is to have one wide colored stripe (exactly like the band of officers' forage caps) and a red edge on both sides of the stripe. The width of the colored stripe is prescribed to be 5/8 vershok [1 1/10 inches], with 1/16 vershok [1/10 inch] of that, on both sides, being occupied by the edge (in those regiments in which such are prescribed for forage cap bands). Between the wide stripe and the separate edges is a space of 1/4 vershok [7/16 inch] The overall width of the edges is 1/16 vershok [1/10 inch]. Along the front edge of the shabrack and along the upper and side edges of the pistol holders only one red piping is prescribed (Illus. 647) [65].

3 January 1853 - Noncombatant lower ranks with **frock coats** are to have these reach to the lower part of the knee [66].

18 February 1854 - The **saddles** of field-grade officers, and likewise regimental and battalion adjutants, are to have a valise [*chemodan*] and greatcoat, as explained above (see Grenadier regiments) [67].

29 April 1854 - Generals and field and company-grade officers are to have, in wartime, **campaign greatcoats** [*pokhodnyya shineli*] of the pattern established at this time for Grenadier regiments (Illus. 648) [68].

14 May 1854 - In the 5th Replacement Battalion [*5-i zapasnyi batalion*] of the L.-Gds. Pavlovsk Regiment the **pompons** on grenadier caps aare ordered to be: in the grenadier platoon—red, in the rifle platoon—yellow, and in the fusilier companies—white, all with light green in the center [69].

16 June 1854 - Fifth replacement [*zapasnyi*] battalions are to have dark-green piping around the top of the **forage cap** [70].

15 September 1854 - In the 6th Replacement Battalion [*6-i zapasnyi batalion*] of the L.-Gds. Pavlovsk Regiment the **pompons** on grenadier caps aare ordered to be: in the grenadier platoon—red, in the rifle platoon—yellow, and in the remaining companies—white, all with light green in the center [71].

13 February 1855 - Approval is given to a description of a new manner of fitting the **firing-cap pouch** [*kapsyulnaya sumochka*], as set forth above for Grenadier regiments [72].

25 - GUARDS LIGHT INFANTRY [*GVARDEISKAYA LEGKAYA PEKHOTA*].

11 February 1826 - Officers in Guards light infantry regiments, in place of their dark-green pants with high boots, and lower combatant ranks in place of their pants with knee gaiters [*kragi*], are ordered to have long dark-green **pants** [*pantalony*] of the pattern introduced at this time for the army, with red piping on the side seams as before for the Jäger and Finland regiments, and yellow for the Volynia Regiment (Illus. 649 and 650). Lower ranks at all times, but company-grade officers when in formation and whenever wearing the sash, are to wear black cloth **half-gaiters** [*polushiblety*] under these pants and over the boots, fastened with five or six small metal buttons the same color as those on the coat. Generals (when in regimental uniform), field-grade officers, and adjutants, while wearing the same pants as for company-grade officers with the troops, are ordered not to have boots with the spurs driven in, and not to wear gaiters. Along with these changes, the horizontal **belt for the knapsack** is to be above the lower buttons on the front of the coat, while the **greatcoat** is carried on the knapsack rolled into a tube in its special oilskin case made of raven's-duck. Clerks and all noncombatant lower ranks in general are ordered to wear grey riding trousers [*reituzy*] without stripes [73].

10 May 1826 - Generals, field-grade officers, and adjutants, when mounted in formation [*v stroyu*] during the summer, are to wear **white linen pants** [*belyya polotnyanyya pantalony*] without integral spats [*kozyrki*], of the same pattern as previously prescribed for the dark-green ones (Illus. 651). In addition, **suede pants** [*zamshevyya pantalony*] of the same pattern may be worn instead of the linen pants [74].

15 September 1826 - Lower ranks who have served out the regulation number of years for retirement without reproach, yet voluntarily remain in service, are ordered to wear a **gold galloon chevron** [*nashivka iz zolotago galuna*] on the left sleeve above and in addition to the yellow tape chevrons [*nashivki iz zheltago basona*] prescribed on 29 March 1825 [75].

12 December 1826 - Officers' rapiers [*shpagi*] are replaced by **half-sabers** [*polusabli*] of the same pattern as those introduced on 20 August 1830 for Army infantry and described above for Grenadier regiments (Illus. 651) [76].

1 January 1827 - Officers' epaulettes are to have little forged or stamped **stars** [*kovannyya zvezdochki*] **as rank distinctions**. These are silver in the Life-Guards Jäger and Finland regiments, and gold in the Volhynia Regiment. Ensigns [*praporshchiki*] have one, Sublieutenants [*Podporuchiki*] two, Lieutenants [*Poruchiki*] three, Staff-Captains [*Stabs-Kapitany*] four, Major Generals [*General-Maiory*] two, and Lieutenant Generals [*General-Leitenanty*] three. Colonels [*Polkovniki*] and full Generals [*polnye Generaly*] are not prescribed any stars [77].

14 February 1827 - In the **Life-Guards Finland Regiment** cuff flaps, instead of being dark green with red piping, are ordered to be red without piping (Illus. 652) [78].

31 July 1827 - Numbers and letters on **shako** and**cartridge -pouch covers**, instead of being of yellow cloth, are ordered to be painted on with yellow oil paint [79].

14 December 1827 - The **chevrons** established on 15 September 1826 for the left sleeves of lower ranks are ordered to be gold or silver, according to the non-commissioned officers' galloon in that regiment in which the man who has served out the regulation number of years for retirement voluntarily remains in service [80].

24 March 1828 - The **coats** of lower ranks are not to be tailored with cinches [*peretyazhki*] [81].

24 April 1828 - The following changes were made in articles of uniform and accouterments:

1.) A new model **shako** [*kiver*]: 5 1/2 vershoks [9 5/8 inches] high with a top diameter not less than 5 5/8 vershoks [9 7/8 inches] and not more than 6 vershoks [10 1/2 inches]. The lower diameter is according to the size of the head. The thickness of the upper, lacquered edge is 5/16 vershok [1/2 inch] (Illus. 653 and 654).

2.) With the increase in the shako's height, the **shako plate** [*gerb*] will be of a new, slightly altered form: in the Jäger and Finland regiments—with an image of St. George the Bearer of Victory and in the Volhynia Regiment—with an image of a Lithuanian horseman within an eagle's shield.

3.) The **shako cords** [*etishket*] are also of a new pattern, consisting of a white cord around the top of the shako and tassels with bows [*banty*] hanging down on the right even with the lower edge of the shako. For privates these last are completely white and for non-commissioned officers white with orange and black.

4.) The **pouch belt** [*perevyaz'*] and **sword-belt** [*portupeya*] are prescribed to be 2 vershoks [3 1/2 inches] wide; the **shoulder belts for the knapsack** [*rantsevye plechevye remni*] — 1 1/2 vershoks [2 5/8 inches]; and the **belt across the chest** [*nagrudnyi remen*] — 1 1/8 vershoks [2 inches].

5.) **Knapsacks** are to be of calfskin [*telyachaya kozha*] as before but with black leather trim (Illus. 653). The knapsack is prescribed to be 9 vershoks [15 3/4 inches] broad, 8 vershoks [14 inches] high, and 2 1/2 vershoks [4 3/8 inches] wide. The length of the cover from the upper edge is 6 vershoks [10 1/2]inches.

6.) In place of their grey coats [*mundiry*], all **non-combatant non-commissioned officers** are issued dark-green **frock coats** [*syurtuki*] with a single row of buttons and the same collar, cuffs, and shoulder straps as for combatant personnel. **Pants**, however, are grey with red piping on the side seams.

7.) **Non-combatant craftsmen** [*masterovye*] of the lower ranks, as well as **medical orderlies** [*lazaretnye sluzhiteli*] are to replace their coats with grey cloth **jackets** [*kurtki*] modeled on the coat, while pants are to be as for the non-combatants above [82].

18 May 1829 - Non-commissioned officers who have been recommended by higher command for promotion to officer rank by virtue of years of service are permitted to have a **silver sword knot** [*serebryanyi temlyak*] [83].

26 December 1829 - All ranks are ordered to have the **buttons** on their coats, frock coats, and greatcoats made with the raised image of a the two-headed eagle prescribed for the shako plate [84].

19 July 1831 - The **Life-Guards Volhynia Regiment** is ordered to have red cuff flaps on the coat instead of yellow (Illus. 655), and in the eagle's shield on buttons and the shako plate, instead of the image of a Lithuanian horseman there is to be an image of St. George the Bearer of Victory [85].

1 January 1832 - Generals who have the diamond-studded **gold rapiers** [*shpagi*] "*za khrabost*" ["for courage"] are not to use **sword knots** with these swords [86].

24 March 1832 - In the **Life-Guards Volhynia Regiment** greatcoat collars are ordered to have button holes of red cloth, with a coat button, after the example of the Life-Guards Finland Regiment (Illus. 656) [87].

8 June 1832 - Officers are permitted to wear **moustaches** [88].

3 January 1833 - Cloth **half-gaiters** [*polushtiblety*] are abolished for company-grade officers and lower ranks, as are shako covers, cartridge-pouch covers, and sword knots for non-commissioned officers and privates (Illus. 657). The latter are to be worn only by those non-commissioned officers have received them in silver [89].

20 January 1833 - Shako covers are left as before [90].

20 February 1833 - All combatant ranks are given new pattern **summer pants** [*pantalony*] or **breeches** [*bryuki*], without buttons or integral spats [*kozyrki*] (Illus. 658), and from this year on drum majors in all three regiments of Guards Light Infantry are given red horse-hair plumes for their shakos, with a white top with an orange stripe in it (Illus. 659) [91].

26 September 1834 - Lower combatant ranks are directed to wear the **knapsack** on two belts lying crosswise over the chest (Illus. 660) [92].

20 August 1835 - It is ordered that:

1.) Officers wear the **knapsack** using only two shoulder belts without any horizontal strap over the chest. These belts are to be lacquered.

2.) For lower ranks a **linen case** [*kholshchevyi chekhol*] or pocket [*karman*] for the forage cap is to be put on the outside of the knapsack on the side that lies on the soldier's back. These cases are to be made from the linings of wornout coats.

3.) For drummers the **knapsack** is to have one belt as before, worn over the left shoulder [93].

31 January 1836 - Lower ranks' **greatcoats** [shineli] are to have nine buttons instead of ten: six along the front opening, two on the shoulder straps, and one on the flap behind [94].

27 April 1836 - **Pompons** are to be lined with black leather [95].

13 May 1836 - **Girths** [podprugi] for officers' saddles are to be dark green with red stripes [96].

21 October 1836 - **Shako plumes** [kivernye sultany] in carabineer platoons and for musicians are to be 11 vershoks [19 1/4 inches] high from the triangular socket to the top, with an upper circumference of 5 2/3 vershoks [10 inches] and a lower one of 4 vershoks [7 inches]. Its weight is to be not more than 54 zolotniks [8 1/10 ounces] [97].

14 January 1837 - Handles of **entrenching tools** [shantsovye instrumenty] are no longer to be painted with oil-based paint, but rather the wood is to be varnished [pokryvat lakom], and directives for carrying and fitting these tools are confirmed, as described above in detail for Grenadier regiments [98].

15 July 1837 - Officers are given a new pattern of **sash** [sharf] that instead of the previous wide lace has narrow, silver lace with three stripes of light-orange and black silk, and is tied with its entire width between the two lower buttons of the coat, as described above in detail for Grenadier regiments [sic, there are no additional details - M.C.] [99].

17 December 1837 - In order to introduce uniformity to officers' **epaulettes**, their pattern is confirmed with the addition of a fourth, narrow braid [uzkii vitok], as described above in detail for Grenadier regiments [sic, there are no additional details - M.C.] [100].

17 January 1838 - In summer, regimental **staff-hornists** [shtab-gornisty], when obliged to be mounted in formation, are ordered to wear winter trousers [bryuki]. Instead of knapsacks they are to have valises [chemodany] of the cavalry pattern and their horses are to be with bridles [uzdechki], with a saddle patterned after the one for mounted artillerymen, without a shabrack or saddlecloth [cheprak ili val'trap] [101].

4 January 1839 - Generals and field and company-grade officers are not to have any bows or bands [banty] on the front of their **pants** or **trousers**. These are to be worn completely smooth in the manner prescribed for lower ranks [102].

16 March 1839 - Lower ranks' **pouch belts** [perevyazi] and **sword belts** [portupei], which were originally 2 1/8 vershoks [3 7/8 inches] wide and then, since 1828, 2 vershoks [3 1/2 inches] wide, are ordered to be 1 1/2 vershoks [2 5/8 inches] wide. **Drummers' crossbelts** [barabannyya perevyazi] are as before, 2 1/2 vershoks [4 2/5 inches] wide [103].

16 October 1840 - Lower ranks who have earned the right to discharge on indefinite leave [bezsrochnyi otpusk] but who voluntarily remain on active service after serving the regulation number of years are to be given **gold or silver galloon chevrons** [shevrony ili nashivki, iz zolotago ili serebryanago galuna], according to the color of the buttons, for the left sleeve, one for every five years of extra service. On this same basis these same chevrons are prescribed for non-commissioned officers who have declined promotion to officer rank and are receiving two-thirds of an ensign's pay, upon serving five or more years after declining such promotion [104].

23 January 1841 - The capes [bolshie vorotniki] of officers' **greatcoats** are to be 1 arshin [28 inches] long as measured from the lower edge of the collar [malyi vorotnik] [105].

8 April 1843 - There are the following changes:

1.) Officers and lower ranks are given a new model **shako** [kiver], 4 3/4 vershoks [8 1/3 inches] high and curving slightly inward toward the bottom. New dimensions are prescribed for shako **plumes**: 9 3/4 vershoks [17 inches] high from the socket to the top, an upper circumference of 5 1/4 vershoks [9 1/4 inches], and a lower circumference of 3 1/2 vershoks [6 1/8 inches] [106].

2.) In order to more easily be distinguished from generals' epaulettes, it is directed that **drum-majors' epaulettes** [tambur-mazhorskie epolety] have red silk mixed in the gold braided threads and in the hanging fringe.

3.) **Rank distinctions** for lower ranks in the Guards light infantry are established in the form of trim sewn onto shoulder straps [nashivki na plechevykh pogonakh], as described above for regiments of the Guards heavy infantry [107].

10 May 1843 - The covers of **cartridge-pouches** [patronnyya sumki] are not to have any break on top [bez pereloma vverkhu], and are to measure [with the cover sewn onto the body of the pouch]: length — 5 vershoks [8 3/4 inches], width at the top edge — 5 1/2 vershoks [9 5/8 inches], width at the bottom edge — 6 vershoks [10 1/2 inches] [108].

2 January 1844 - Officers are to have an oblong, metal **cockade** [kokarda] on the front of the band of their forage caps, in the same colors as the cockade on officers' hats [109].

8 January 1844 - **Staff-hornists** [shtab-gornisty], when mounted in formation, are permitted to have spurs [110].

14

8 May 1844 - It is directed that shakos [*kivera*] be replaced by **helmets** [*kaski*] of black lacquered leather, with two visors, mountings of the same color as the buttons, a horsehair plume [*sultan*] (red for musicians and black for other personnel), and the previous shako plate, all of the pattern of the helmets introduced at this time in the Guards heavy infantry (Illus. 661 and 662) [111].

20 May 1844 - A new scheme for lower ranks' **forage caps** is approved, on the basis of which the piping on the upper edge is to be: in the 1st battalion—red, in the 2nd—white, and in the 3rd—blue [*svetlosinii*].

The cap band colors remain as before, dark green with two rows of piping in the Jäger and Finland regiments, but dark green with two rows of yellow piping in the Volhynia regiment. Company numbers and Cyrillic letters are cut out as before, on yellow cloth. For officers of the first two regiments the piping on the top edge of the forage cap is red, but yellow in the third [112].

17 November 1844 - Instructions for storing and protecting the **helmet plume** [*kasochnyi sultan*] are approved, as set forth in detail above for Grenadier regiments [113].

7 December 1844 - Generals who are wearing a regimental coat [*polkovoi mundir*] when not on duty are to have a **white plume** [*sultan*] on the hat [*shlyapa*] instead of a black one [114].

4 January 1845 - Officers' helmets are to have, on the right side under the chin-scales, a metal **cockade** patterned after the one worn on the hat [115].

9 August 1845 - The **plume** is not to be worn with helmets while in camp dress [*pre lagernoi forme*], even if those personnel entitled to plumes are wearing coats [*mundiry*] (Illus. 663) [116].

26 April 1846 - Instead of a brass spear point, **unit guidons** [*zhalonerskie znaki*] are to have a brass ball [117].

23 June 1846 - With the introduction of percussion-lock weapons, a description for fitting the **firing-cap pouch** [*kapsyulnaya sumka*] is approved, as laid out in detail for Grenadier regiments [118].

19 May 1847 - Noncombatant lower ranks are given the same **forage caps** as prescribed at this time in the heavy Guards infantry, but in the L.-Gds. Volhynia Regiment with yellow piping instead of red [119].

29 November 1847 - **Distinguished officer candidates** [*portupei-praporshchikam i portupei-yunkeram*] who, based on the regulations concerning the acceptance of young noblemen for service in the Guards, carry out officers' responsibilities in their regiments after passing an examination, are ordered to wear an officer's **half-saber** [*poulsablya*] instead of a short sword [*tesak*] [120].

9 January 1848 - On those days when they are obliged to remain in ceremonial dress [*prazdnichnaya forma*] after the mounting of the guard [*posle razvoda*], generals and field and company-grade officers are permitted to wear the **frock coat** with helmet and plume for walking-out [121].

19 April 1849 - With the introduction of new **English signal bugles** [*Angliiskie signalnye rozhki*], the means of fitting a strap to them is established, as described in detail for Grenadier regiments [122].

14 September 1849 - Approval is given as to the type of **percussion pistol** [*udarnyi pistolet*] for officers, as related above for Grenadier regiments [123].

9 and 25 November 1849 - The manner of fitting the **helmet** is confirmed (see Grenadier regiments) [124].

17 December 1849 - In Guards Jäger regiments, it is ordered to have **three grenades** on **drummers' crossbelts**, after the example of other regiments of Guards infantry (Illus. 664) [125].

24 December 1849 - The grip on the hilt of the **gold half-saber** awarded for bravery is to be gold [126].

17 January 1851 - Approval is given to a description of the manner of gathering up and folding back the skirts [*poly*] of the **greatcoat** (see Grenadier regiments) [127].

8 July 1851 - The frizzen cover [*polunagalishche*] is withdrawn and approval is given to patterns and descriptions of the **infantry drum** [*pekhotnyi baraban*], **water flask** [*vodonosnaya flyaga*], **greatcoat strap** [*shinelnyi remen'*], **sword belt** [*portupeya*], **crossbelt** [*perevyaz'*], and **cover for the nipple of percussion weapons** [*chekhol na sterzhen' dlya udarnykh ruzhei*] (see Guards heavy infantry) [128].

20 October 1851 - Approval is given to the list and description of items that the soldier is to have in his **knapsack** (see Grenadier regiments) [129].

26 January 1852 - Noncombatant lower ranks with **forage caps** of grey cloth are to have a cap band in the color of the collar of the regiment or unit to which they belong (Illus. 665) [130].

17 October 1852 - Generals, field and company-grade officers, and adjutants are ordered to have when in formation: for parade uniform a shabrack of the previous pattern, and for campaign uniform the newly introduced ***vice-shabrack***

[vitse-cheprak] as established for Guards Heavy Infantry, except that for the L.-Gds. Volhynia Regiment the edges on the vice-shabrack are to be yellow (Illus. 666) (131).

3 January 1853 - Noncombatant lower ranks are ordered to have their **frock coats** reach to the lower part of the knee (132).

18 February 1854 - The **saddles** of field-grade officers, and likewise regimental and battalion adjutants, are to have a valise [chemodan] and greatcoat, following the directives set forth above (see Grenadier regiments) (133).

29 April 1854 - Generals and field and company-grade officers are to have, in wartime, **campaign greatcoats** [pokhodnyya shineli] (see Grenadier regiments) (134).

16 June 1854 - Fifth replacement [zapasnyi] battalions are to have dark-green piping around the top of the **forage cap** (135).

13 February 1855 - Approval is given to a description of a new manner of fitting the **firing-cap pouch** [kapsyulnaya sumochka] (see Grenadier regiments) (136).

26 - LIFE-GUARDS FINNISH RIFLE BATTALION [LEIB-GVARDII FINNSKII STRELKOVYI BATALION].

16 July 1829 - The **Life-Guards Finnish Rifle Battalion**, renamed from the Finnish Instructional Rifle Battalion and included in the Young Guard [molodaya Gvardiya], is prescribed uniform clothing as for the regiments of Guards Light Infantry (the Jäger, Finland, and Volhynia regiments) but with blue [svetlosinii] cloth piping, cuff flaps, shoulder straps, and the field on officers' epaulettes, with white buttons and button hole loops (silver for officers). Lower ranks' buttons have a single-flame grenade on them instead of a two-headed eagle which is only prescribed for officers, and the shako plate is the coat of arms of the Grand Duchy of Finland [Velikoe Knyazhestvo Finlyandskoe] on a eagle's shield, and this is on officers' gorgets as well as on shakos and officers' buttons (Illus. 667 and 668). This coat of arms depicts a lion holding a saber in its front paws, surrounded by stars (Illus. 669). Instead of muskets and the normal short sword, this battalion is given rifles [shtutsera] and detachable short swords [s"emnye tesaki], like those described above for the Grenadier Sapper Battalion and other Sapper battalions (137).

3 September 1829 - In the **Life-Guards Finnish Rifle Battalion** it is ordered to have:

a) On the badges for cartridge pouches, instead of the previous Latin letters—the Russian letter: L. G. F. S.

b) On shako and pouch covers, instead of the *Latin* letter, signifying the initial letter of the word *Compagnie* (company)—the Russian letter R [rota], and

c) After the example of Young Guard regiments, on non-commissioned officers' and musicians' coats—galloon, the same color as the buttons (138).

8 June 1832 - Officers are permitted to wear **moustaches** (139).

3 January 1833 - Cloth **half-gaiters** [polushtiblety] are abolished for company-grade officers and lower ranks, as are shako covers and cartridge-pouch covers for non-commissioned officers and privates (140).

20 January 1833 - **Shako covers** are left as before (141).

20 February 1833 - All combatant ranks are given new pattern **summer pants** [pantalony] or **breeches** [bryuki], without buttons or integral spats [kozyrki] (Illus. 670) (142).

31 July 1834 - Lower ranks' **buttons** are ordered to have the image of a two-headed eagle, as for the battalion's officers up to this time (143).

26 September 1834 - Lower combatant ranks are directed to wear the **knapsack** on two belts lying crosswise over the chest (Illus. 671) (144).

20 August 1835 - It is ordered that:

1.) Officers wear the **knapsack** using only two shoulder belts without any horizontal strap over the chest (Illus. 672).

2.) For lower ranks a **linen case** [kholshchevyi chekhol] or pocket [karman] for the forage cap is to be put on the outside of the knapsack on the side that lies on the soldier's back (145).

31 January 1836 - Lower ranks' **greatcoats** [shineli] are to have nine buttons instead of ten: six along the front opening, two on the shoulder straps, and one on the flap behind (146).

27 April 1836 - **Pompons** are to be lined with black leather (147).

13 May 1836 - **Girths** [podprugi] for officers' saddles are to be dark green with red stripes (148).

14 January 1837 - Handles of **entrenching tools** [shantsovye instrumenty] are no longer to be painted with oil-based paint, but rather the wood is to be varnished [pokryvat lakom], and directives for carrying and fitting these tools are confirmed, as described above in detail for Grenadier regiments (149).

15 July 1837 - Officers are given a new pattern of **sash** [*sharf*] that instead of the previous wide lace has narrow, silver lace with three stripes of light-orange and black silk, and is tied with its entire width between the two lower buttons of the coat, as described above in detail for Grenadier regiments [sic, there are no additional details - M.C.] (150).

17 December 1837 - In order to introduce uniformity to officers' **epaulettes**, their pattern is confirmed with the addition of a fourth, narrow braid [*uzkii vitok*], as described above in detail for Grenadier regiments [sic, there are no additional details - M.C.] (151).

4 January 1839 - Generals and field and company-grade officers are not to have any bows or bands [*banty*] on the front of their **pants** or **trousers**. These are to be worn completely smooth in the manner prescribed for lower ranks (152).

16 March 1839 - Lower ranks' **pouch belts** [*perevyazi*] and **sword belts** [*portupei*], which since 1828 were originally 2 ver-shoks [3 1/2 inches] wide, are ordered to be 1 1/2 vershoks [2 5/8 inches] wide (153).

23 January 1841 - The capes [*bolshie vorotniki*] of officers' **greatcoats** are to be 1 arshin [28 inches] long as measured from the lower edge of the collar [*malyi vorotnik*] (154).

8 April 1843 - Officers and lower ranks are given a new model **shako** [*kiver*], curving slightly inward toward the bottom (Illus. 673). Sergeants [*fel'dfebeli*], non-commissioned officers [*unter-ofitsery*], and corporals [*yefreitory*] are given rank distinctions for the shoulder straps. Both these items are identical with those established at this time for Guards infantry regiments and described above (155).

10 May 1843 - The covers of **cartridge-pouches** [*patronnyya sumki*] are not to have any break on top [*bez pereloma vverkhu*], and are to measure [with the cover sewn onto the body of the pouch]: length — 5 vershoks [8 3/4 inches], width at the top edge — 5 1/2 vershoks [9 5/8 inches], width at the bottom edge — 6 vershoks [10 1/2 inches] (156).

3 August 1843 - To encourage battalion lower ranks who continually distinguish themselves in marksmanship, it is ordered to give them sewn-on pieces of **galloon** [*nashivki*]: for non-commissioned officers on the shoulder straps, and for riflemen [*strelki*] around the coat's cuffs, after the manner established for bombardiers in the Artillery (157).

2 January 1844 - Officers are to have an oblong, metal **cockade** [*kokarda*] on the front of the band of their forage caps, in the same colors as the cockade on officers' hats (158).

9 May 1844 - It is directed that shakos [*kivera*] be replaced by **helmets** [*kaski*] of black lacquered leather, with two visors, metal mountings of the same color as the buttons, a horsehair plume [*sultan*] (red for musicians and black for other personnel), and the previous shako plate. The helmets are of the pattern introduced at this time in the the rest of the Guards infantry (Illus. 674) (159).

20 May 1844 - A new scheme for lower ranks' **forage caps** is approved, on the basis of which it remains as before, dark green with three blue [*svetlosinii*] lines of piping (160).

17 November 1844 - Instructions for storing and protecting the **helmet plume** [*kasochnyi sultan*] are approved, as set forth in detail above for Grenadier regiments (161).

4 January 1845 - Officers' helmets are to have, on the right side under the chin-scales, a metal **cockade** patterned after the one worn on the hat (Illus. 675) (162).

9 August 1845 - The **plume** is not to be worn with helmets while in camp dress [*pre lagernoi forme*], even if those personnel entitled to plumes are wearing coats [*mundiry*] (Illus. 676) (163).

Besides the uniform changes described here, in 1842 the battalion received by HIGHEST Order a second complement [*komplekt*] of **rifles** from the Liège factory in Belgium (Illus. 677), to be used only for target practice and when on campaign (164).

23 June 1846 - A description for fitting the **firing-cap pouch** [*kapsyulnaya sumka*] is approved (see Grenadier regiments) (165).

19 May 1847 - Noncombatant lower ranks are given **forage caps** of grey cloth with blue [*svetlosinii*] piping (166).

29 November 1847 - **Distinguished officer candidates** [*portupei-praporshchikam i portupei-yunkeram*] who carry out officers' responsibilities are ordered to wear an officer's **half-saber** [*poulsablya*] instead of a short sword [*tesak*] (167).

9 January 1848 - On those days when ceremonial dress [*prazdnichnaya forma*] is the designated uniform after the mounting of the guard [*posle razvoda*], generals and field and company-grade officers are permitted to wear the **frock coat** with helmet and plume for walking-out (168).

19 April 1849 - With the introduction of new **English signal bugles** [*Angliiskie signalnye rozhki*], the means of fitting a strap to them is confirmed (see Grenadier regiments) (Illus. 678) (169).

14 September 1849- Approval is given as to the pattern of **percussion pistol** [*udarnyi pistolet*] for officers (see Grenadier regiments) (170).

9 and 25 November 1849 - The manner of fitting the **helmet** is confirmed (see Grenadier regiments) [171].

24 December 1849 - The grip on the hilt of the **gold half-saber** awarded for bravery is to be gold [172].

17 January 1851 - Approval is given to a description of the manner of gathering up and folding back the skirts [poly] of the **greatcoat** (see Grenadier regiments) [173].

8 July 1851 - Approval is given to patterns and descriptions of the **infantry drum** [pekhotnyi baraban], **water flask** [vodonosnaya flyaga], **greatcoat strap** [shinelnyi remen'], **sword belt** [portupeya], and **crossbelt** [perevyaz'] (see Guards heavy infantry) [174].

20 October 1851 - Approval is given to the list and description of items that the soldier is to have in his **knapsack** (see Grenadier regiments) [175].

26 January 1852 - Noncombatant lower ranks are to have a cap band on their grey **forage caps** the same color as the collar in the battalion [176].

28 December 1852 - Generals, field and company-grade officers, and adjutants are ordered to have when in formation: for parade uniform a shabrack of the previous pattern, and for campaign uniform a **vice-shabrack** [vitse-cheprak] of the pattern for regiments of Guards Light Infantry, except that the red edges are changed to blue [svetlsinii] [177].

3 January 1853 - Noncombatant lower ranks are ordered to have their **frock coats** reach to the lower part of the knee [178].

18 February 1854 - The **saddles** of field-grade officers, and likewise regimental and battalion adjutants, are to have a valise [chemodan] and greatcoat, as related above for Grenadier regiments [179].

29 April 1854 - Generals and field and company-grade officers are to have, in wartime, **campaign greatcoats** [pokhodnyya shineli] (see Grenadier regiments) [180].

13 February 1855 - Approval is given to a description of a new manner of fitting the **firing-cap pouch** [kapsyulnaya sumochka] (see Grenadier regiments) [181].

27 - GUARDS CUIRASSIER REGIMENTS [GVARDEISKIE KIRASIRSKIE POLKI].

11 February 1826 - Generals and field and company-grade officers of the Cavalier Guards, Life-Guards Horse, Life-Guards Cuirassier, Life-Guards Podolia Cuirassier, and HER MAJESTY'S Leib-Cuirassier regiments are to have riding grey **riding trousers** [reituzy, from the German Reithosen - M.C.] when wearing the dark-green undress coat [vitse-mundir], with wide stripes [lampasy] the same color as the facing on the kolet coat (Illus. 679). The same riding trousers are prescribed for clerks and in general all non-combatant lower ranks [182].

25 June 1826 - Officers of **HER MAJESTY'S Leib-Cuirassier Regiment** are ordered to have button-hole lace [petlitsy] on the collars and cuffs of their kolet coats and white undress coats, as are lower ranks on their coats: silver for former and of white lace [tes'ma] for the latter (Illus. 680) [183].

15 September 1826 - Lower ranks who have served out the regulation number of years without reproach and who voluntarily remain on service are to wear **gold galloon** sewn onto the left sleeve, as described above for Grenadier regiments [184].

1 January 1827 - In order to distinguish rank, officers' **epaulettes** are to have small forged and stamped stars, of the same appearance and according to the same scheme as related above for Army cavalry regiments [185].

9 May 1827 - For officers and lower ranks of all five regiments are given a new style of **plumage** [plyumazh], thicker and longer than before, and the height of the helmet itself is decreased (Illus. 681) [186].

14 December 1827 - The **lace** [nashivka] sewn onto lower ranks' left sleeves, instituted on 15 September 1826, is to be either gold or silver according to the color of the non-commissioned officers' lace in the regiment in which the man who served out the regulation number of years for retirement voluntarily remains in service [187].

11 February 1828 - For the Cavalier Guards, Life-Guards Horse, Life-Guards Cuirassier, Life-Guards Podolia Cuirassier, and HER MAJESTY'S Leib-Cuirassier regiments it is ordered that **pouches** [podsumki] be worn on the right side, and that **bandoleers** [panatlery] and **carbine hooks** be abolished except for carbineers, who are to wear them over the pouch belt after the example of carbineers in the Light cavalry (Illus. 682) [188].

24 March 1828 - Lower ranks are forbidden to have cinches on their **coats** [mundiry] [189].

24 April 1828 - Instead of the grey coats [mundiry serago sveta] previously used by them, all non-combatant non-commissioned officers throughout are given dark-green **frock coats** with one row of buttons [temnozelenye, odnobortnye syurtuki] and the same collar, cuffs, and shoulder straps as for combatants, while the pants are grey with piping on the side seams in the same color as the collar. Instead of their previous coats [mundiry], non-combatant master-craftsmen lower ranks

18

[*masterovye nestroevye nizhnie chiny*], as well as infirmary orderlies [*lazaretynye sluzhiteli*], are to wear jackets [*kurtki*] of grey cloth, with distinctions as on the coats, with pants as for the preceding non-combatants [190].

In this same year, the Cavalier Guards, Life-Guards Horse, Life-Guards Cuirassier, Life-Guards Podolia Cuirassier, and HER MAJESTY'S Leib-Cuirassier regiments were given brass **cuirasses** in place of the previous black ones (Illus. 683 and 684). Along with this, in all five regiments the previous broadswords [*palashi*] with two arches [*duzhki*] in the guard are replaced by new ones with three arches, identical to those introduced in Army Cuirassier regiments in 1826 [191].

9 July 1829 - The wide stripes [*lampasy*] on officers' and lower ranks' **riding trousers** [*reituzy*] are abolished, and only one row of piping is left, on the side seams [192].

26 December 1829 - All combatant ranks are ordered to have uniform **buttons** with the raised image of a two-headed eagle: in the Cavalier Guards, Life-Guards Horse, Life-Guards Cuirassier, and HER MAJESTY'S Leib-Cuirassier regiments—with an image of St. George the Bearer of Victory, but in the Life-Guards Podolia Cuirassiers—with an image of a Lithuanian horseman [193].

31 May 1830 - Lower ranks of the Life-Guards Horse Regiment and the Life-Guards Podolia Cuirassier Regiment, in place of their previous smocks [*kiteli*], are issued dark-green cloth **jackets** [*kurtki*], without tails, but with a single row of the same buttons as on the *kolet* coat, piping on the collar, cuffs, and shoulder straps: red in the Horse Regiment and yellow in the Podolia Regiment [194].

28 June 1830 - Officers of the Cavalier Guards and Life-Guards Horse regiments, when in their red coats with sash, and the Life-Guards Cuirassier and HER MAJESTY'S Leib-Cuirassier regiments, when in their white coats with sash, are ordered to wear the **broadsword** [*palash*]. With the same coats but without the sash, they are to wear the **rapier** [*shpaga*]. When in dark-green undress coats [*vitse-mundiry*] with sash and duty requires them to be in helmets with pouches— broadswords, and in other situations, even though they are wearing the sash—rapiers [195].

5 July 1830 - In the Life-Guards Cuirassier Regiment smocks are replaced by **jackets**, identical to those introduced on 31 May for the Life-Guards Horse and Life-Guards Podolia Cuirassier regiments, but with blue [*svetlosinii*] piping on the collar, cuffs, and shoulder straps [196].

24 September 1830 - The lining [*podkladka*] of officers' **frock coats** [*syurtuki*] is to be white [197].

22 August 1831 - **HIS MAJESTY'S Life-Guards Cuirassier Regiment**, formed from the Life-Guards Cuirassier and Life-Guards Podolia Cuirassier regiments, is ordered upon its inclusion in the Old Guard to have the button-hole lace on lower ranks' *kolet* coats and the lace [*tes'ma*] on shabracks and pistol holders in yellow instead of white (Illus. 685) [198].

8 December 1831 - The front ranks of squadrons are to have **lances** [*piki*] with shafts finished with oil paint of the same color as the shabrack: in HER MAJESTY'S Cavalier Guards Regiment—red, Life-Guards Horse Regiment—dark blue [*temnosinii*], HER MAJESTY'S Life-Guards Cuirassier Regiment—blue [*svetlosinii*], and The HEIR AND TSESAREVICH'S Leib-Cuirassier Regiment—raspberry. These lances are to have **pennons** [*flyugera*] divided into three parts, of the following colors: for the Life-Guards Horse—upper part yellow, lower blue [*svetlosinii*], middle white; for HER MAJESTY'S Life-Guards Cuirassiers—upper and lower parts blue [*svetlosinii*], middle white; for HEIR AND TSESAREVICH'S Leib-Cuirassier Regiment—upper and lower parts raspberry, and middle white [199].

1 January 1832 - Generals who have **gold swords**, decorated with diamonds and with the inscription *"Za khrabost"* ["For courage"], are to wear these without swordknots [200].

21 May 1832 - For lower ranks of HER MAJESTY'S Cavalier Guards Regiment an everyday single-breasted **undress coat** [*vitse-mundir*] is confirmed, of dark-green cloth, with long tails and the same collar, cuffs, shoulder straps, and buttons as on the *kolet* coat, as well as the same red piping on the collar, cuffs, and shoulder straps, down the front opening, and on the turnbacks and pocket flaps. [201]

8 June 1832 - Generals and field and company-grade officers are permitted to wear **moustaches** [202].

27 February 1833 - HIS MAJESTY'S Life-Guards Cuirassier Regiment is ordered to have the image of a two-headed eagle on the front part of the **cuirass**: of red copper [*krasnaya med'*] for lower ranks, and gilt for officers (Illus. 687 and 688) [203].

18 November 1833 In The HEIR AND TSESAREVICH'S Leib-Cuirassier Regiment it is ordered that the front of the **cuirass** have an eight-pointed star with a monogram A beneath an IMPERIAL CROWN: of red copper for lower ranks and gilt for officers (Illus. 689 and 690) [204].

15 April 1834 - **Cartridge pouches** [*lyadunki*] and **crossbelts** [*perevyazyi*] are to be of a new pattern, with smaller-sized cover flaps and narrower crossbelts [205].

25 April 1834 - In the **HEIR AND TSESAREVICH'S Leib-Cuirassier Regiment**, the raspberry [*malinovyi*] color in uniforms as well as in shabracks, pistol holders, and lances is changed to blue [*svetlosinii*], and the white color of buttons, trim on shabracks and pistol holders, and in the middle part of lance pennons—to yellow (Illus. 691) [206].

2 May 1834 - In order that **swords** [*palashi*] may be better handled, it is ordered that their hilts [*yefesy*] be reworked so that the straight arch [*pryamaya duzhka*], where it joins the pommel [*golovka*], is sawn off even with the curving part [*sognutaya chast'*], while the grip [*grif*], or wooden handle [*derevyannaya ruchka*], is cut smooth where it is pressed on by the thumb [207].

3 December 1834 - It is ordered that there are to be no **pistols** in Guards Cuirassier regiments [208].

19 December 1834 - The previous adjustable buckle on the **sword belt** is replaced by a plate [*blyakha*] of red copper, with the stamped and raised two-headed eagle (Illus. 692) [209].

4 February 1835 - A new model **helmet** is approved, lower than previously, of the same size as those introduced at this time in Army Cuirassier regiments [210].

20 February 1835 - With **pistols** being withdrawn from Cuirassiers, the former ramrods [*shompola*] over the cartridge pouches [*lyadunki*] are also withdrawn. Along with this, a new pattern of **bandolier** [*pantaler*], or **shoulder belt** [*pogonnaya perevyaz'*], is confirmed for Carabiniers, with brass fittings, an iron hook, and a strap for the ramrod [211].

7 June 1835 - Confirmation is given to the description of the items to be stowed in the **valise** [*chemodan*], **sack** [*sakva*], and **holsters** [*kobury*] that is laid out in detail above for Army Cuirassier regiments [212].

31 January 1836 - Lower ranks' **greatcoats** are to have nine buttons instead of ten, as related above for Guards Heavy Infantry [213].

13 May 1836 - Officers' **saddle girths** [*podprugi*] are to be white with red stripes [214].

15 July 1837 - A new pattern of officer's **sash** is approved, the same as described above for Grenadier regiments [215].

17 December 1837 - A new pattern for officers' **epaulettes** is confirmed, with the addition of a fourth, narrow, twist of braid [216].

26 February 1838 - Trumpeters are to have cloth **shoulder straps** [*pogony*], as other lower ranks (Illus. 693) [217].

27 November 1838 - Carabiniers' **bandoliers** [*pantalery*] in Guards Cuirassier regiments are ordered to be fitted in the style of Light Cavalry, i.e. so that the bandolier belt is longer than the cartridge-pouch belt (Illus. 694) [218], in accordance with the following description approved by HIGHEST AUTHORITY:

1.) The bandolier is worn across the left shoulder, over the cartridge-pouch belt; its width is equal to that of this belt, i.e. 1 1/2 vershoks [2 5/8 inches]. It is made long enough so that when the bandolier is worn and the carbine [*shtutser*] is hanging on its hook, there are 2 vershoks [3 1/2 inches] from the right elbow to the end of the butt.

2.) To the bandolier over the chest, underneath and next to the left shoulder, is sewn a small strap, 4 vershoks [7 inches] long, which is passed through two small holes in the cartridge-pouch belt and tied below.

3.) The end of the bandolier, going from under the right hand to the back, passes through the clasp and bow [*zapryazhnik i pryazhechnaya duzhka*] of the buckle, and being bent downwards near the bow, is tightly sewn to the side facing the back.

4.) The other end of the bandolier, going over the left shoulder, passes through the buckle where it is held by two prongs, and then through the clasp, and a brass endpiece is fastened to the end with a small strap.

5.) The upper edge of the brass buckle is to be no further than 2 vershoks [3 1/2 inches] from the back edge of the left shoulder strap. Likewise, the distance between the buckle and clasp and between the latter and the endpiece is to be no further than 2 vershoks [3 1/2 inches].

4 January 1839 - Generals and field and company-grade officers are not to have any bows or bands on the front of their **riding trousers** and **pants**, but are rather to have them completely smooth, in the manner established for lower ranks [219].

16 October 1840 - The regulation concerning lower ranks' **gold chevrons** [*zolotye shevrony*] is confirmed as laid out above for Grenadier regiments [220].

23 January 1841 - The capes of officers' **greatcoats** are to be 28 inches long as measured from the bottom edge of the collar [221]. In this same year red cloth **supravestes** [*supervesty*] were introduced for use by officers and lower ranks of HER MAJESTY'S Cavalier Guards and Life-Guards Horse regiments assigned to guard duties within the IMPERIAL Palaces, on festive days during HIGHEST appearances. In HER MAJESTY'S Cavalier Guards these supravestes have on the front and back an eight-pointed star with a monogram A under a crown, while in the Life-Guards Horse Regiment a metal image of a two-headed eagle the same color as the buttons. Trim and the toothed edging (blue [*svetlostinii*] in the Cavalier Guards and dark blue [*temnosinii*] in the Life-Guards Horse) are lined with yellow tape [*bason*] for lower ranks and with gallon for officers, the same color as the buttons (Illus. 695 and 696) [222].

31 January 1843 - The **lances** in the regiments are ordered to be reworked according to a new pattern, so that the shaft [*drevko*] with its endpiece [*nakonechnik*] measures 4 1/2 arshins [10 1/2 feet] [223].

8 April 1843 - Lower ranks' leather **sword knots** with woolen tassels are ordered to be replaced with ones that are entirely of leather [224].

On this same date, in order to distinguish **rank** among the lower ranks, it was established that lace [*nashivki*] is to be sewn onto the **shoulder straps** of coats and greatcoats according to the following directions:

1.) For senior sergeants [*starshie vakhtmistry*] - wide gold or silver (according to the color of the buttons) galloon, sewn in one row across the shoulder straps, close to the button hole, as related above for sergeants [*feldfebeli*] of Grenadier regiments.

2.) For distinguished officer candidates [*portupei-yunkera*] and officer candidates [*yunkera*] - narrow gold or silver (according to the color of the buttons) galloon, sewn along the edges of the shoulder strap, as related above for distinguished officer candidates and officer candidates of Grenadier regiments.

3.) For junior sergeants [*mladshchie vakhtmistry*] - narrow woollen lace, in three rows across the shoulder strap, as related above for section non-commission officers of Grenadier regiments.

4.) For non-commissioned officers [*unter-ofitsery*] - the same lace, in two rows, as related above for non-commissioned officers of Grenadier regiments.

5.) For corporals [*yefreitory*] - the same lace, in one row, as related above for corporals in Grenadier regiments [225].

10 May 1843 - Cover flaps [*kryshki*] for **cartridge pouches** are to be (with the cover sewn to the box): 4 1/2 vershoks [8 inches] long, 4 7/8 vershoks [9 inches] wide at the top edge, and 5 5/8 vershoks [10 inches] wide along the bottom edge. The oval belt rings are to be replaced with circular ones. Belts are attached to the stocks of the carbines by means of special straps with buckles, and in order to avoid the upper brass band hitting the spurs, as well as so that the carbines do not drag on the ground when dismounted, they are to be raised up by shortening the bandolier, according to the height of the individual [226].

2 January 1844 - The bands of officers' forage caps are to have **cockades**, as related above for Grenadier regiments (Illus. 697) [227].

2 February 1844 - All sergeants [*vakhtmistry*], non-commissioned officers [*unter-ofitsery*], and trumpeters are to have a single **pistol** in the left holder [*chushka*]. Along with this, trumpeters are given pouches with belts to hold cartridges, as for other lower ranks [228].

19 February 1844 - The shortening of the **bandolier** as established on 10 May 1843, in accordance with an individual's height, is to be done by means of a brass ring on its end, so that below it is even with the lower edge of the cuirass (Illus. 698) [229].

1844 May 20 - A new scheme for the lower ranks' **forage caps** is confirmed, based on which they remain white as before, while the piping around the top is to be: in the 1st double-squadron [*divizion*] - red, in the 2nd - blue [*svetlosinii*], in the 3rd - dark green, and in the replacement [*zapasnyi*] and reserve [*rezervnyi*] - without piping. The cap band is prescribed to be the same color as the coat collar, with two white pipings around both edges, and with the cut-out number of the squadron and the Cyrillic letter *E* [for *eskadron*] on yellow cloth. For officers of all double-squadrons the cap band is the same as the lower ranks', with two white pipings, but without a numeral or letter, while the piping around the top of the forage cap is the same color as the band [230].

21 September 1844 - Non-commissioned officer **standard-bearers** [*shtandartnye unter-ofitsery*] in formation are to always have the **cartridge pouch** beneath the crossbelt for the standard [231].

27 January 1845 - The previous **helmets** with hair combs [*volosyanyi plyumazh*] are replaced by new ones with plumes [*sultany*] of black hair, or red for trumpeters, like those introduced at this time in Army Cuirassier regiments. The helmet plates remain the same (Illus. 699). Along with this, hats are restricted to generals only. On occassions when so ordered, these helmets will have a gilt or silvered two-headed eagle, according to the color of the buttons (Illus. 700 and 701) [232].

29 March 1845 - The black **plumes** prescribed for helmets on 27 January are replaced by white ones (Illus. 702) [233].

15 November 1845 - Guards Cuirassier regiments are ordered to have **pioneer axes** [*shantsovye topory*] and **spades** [*lopaty*], as prescribed at this same time for Army Cuirassier regiments [234].

19 November 1845 - On the **lances**, the clamps [*skoby*] which come out of the sharp upper end piece and blunt lower end piece to hold them to the shaft, as well as the "ears" in which the lance sling [*temlyak*] goes, are to be painted the same color as the shafts, as was done on the lances of the previous pattern [235].

2 February 1846 - Regiments of the Guards Cuirassier Division are to have tombak [*tompakovyi*] **helmets**, as follows: a) in HER MAJESTY'S Cavalier Guards and HIS MAJESTY'S Life-Guards Cuirassier regiments these helmets have grenades, plates, and chin scales of tinned brass [*mednyi luzhenyi*]; b) in the Life-Guards Horse and HIS HIGHNESS THE HEIR AND TSESAREVICH'S Leib-Cuirassier regiments—all the mentioned parts are brass, since the eagles on the helmets in those regiments are prescribed to be gilt; c) in HER MAJESTY'S Cavalier Guards, Life-Guards Horse, and HIS MAJESTY'S Life-Guards Cuirassier regiments the helmets are to have the star of the order of St. Andrew the First Called, with an enamel design in center, while HIS HIGHNESS THE HEIR AND TSESAREVICH'S Leib-Cuirassier Regiment has the same star with the stamped and raised monogram of HIS HIGHNESS in the center; d) on the grenades, the helmets have white horsehair plumes. When not with troop units, officers are allowed to use leather helmets with the previous fittings and a white plume (Illus. 703 and 704) [236].

7 May 1846 - Regiments of the Guards Cuirassier Division are to have **cuirasses** of the same pattern as established for regiments of the 2nd Cuirassier Division (see Army Cuirassier regiments) (Illus. 703 and 704) [237].

13 September 1846 - Officers' **pistols** are to be of the new pattern with a percussion lock, for which new carriers [*kobury*] are approved, made to fit these locks [238].

19 May 1847 - Lower noncombatant ranks are ordered to have the same **forage caps** as prescribed at this time for Guards infantry regiments, but in HIS MAJESTY'S Life-Guards Cuirassier and HIS HIGHNESS THE HEIR AND TSESAREVICH'S Leib-Cuirassier regiments—with blue [*svetlosinii*] piping instead of red [239].

9 January 1848 - Generals and field and company-grade officers, on those days when after guard mount parade uniform is the designated order of dress, they are allowed to wear, for walking out, **frock coats** with riding trousers, along with helmets with plumes (Illus. 704) [240].

19 January 1848 - Confirmation is given to the description of the **firing-cap pouch** [*kapsyulnaya sumochka*] worn with the cartridge pouch (see Army Cuirassier regiments) [241].

25 April 1848 - The **valise's flap** [*klapan na chemodane*] with buttons is completely done away with [242].

31 March 1849 - It is directed that lower ranks' **coats** have small brass hooks so that when riding, the sword belt is not pulled away [243].

24 December 1849 - The grips of **gold swords** awarded for bravery are to be gold [244].

5 March 1850 - Bandoliers [*pantalery*] for standards are ordered to be 2 1/2 vershoks [4 3/8 inches] wide and 2 arshins [56 inches] long. In all regiments the facing side is to be trimmed with velvet: in HER MAJESTY'S Cavalier Guards Regiment—red with silver fittings; in the Life-Guards Horse Regiment—dark blue [*sinii*] with gold fitting; in HIS MAJESTY'S Life-Guards Cuirassier Regiment—blum [*svetlosinii*] with silver fittings; and in HIS HIGHNESS THE HEIR AND TSESAREVICH'S Leib-Cuirassier Regiment—blue [*svetlosinii*] with gold fittings. For all regiments the inner side of the bandoliers is to be lined with white cloth [245].

30 March 1851 - With the introduction of smaller **bandoliers** and **crossbelts** with a movable **firing-cap pouch** fitted onto a small iron hook, a description of these items is approved (see Army Cuirassier regiments) [246].

15 April 1851 - Approval is given to a description for fitting straps to the **valise** for dismounted lower ranks in the Cavalry, and prescribed to also be in effect for personnel released on leave from Cavalry units (see Army Cuirassier regiments) [247].

25 June 1851 - **Generals** of Cuirassier regiments are ordered to never affix stars of orders [*ordenskiya zvezdy*] to their cuirasses as has been done previously, but are rather to wear only orders and badges for distinction [*ordena i znaki otlichiya*] on the cuirasses [248]. [What this regulation says is that only the small crosses of medals and awards are to be worn, and not the associated large stars that are also part of the regalia of an awarded order - M.C.]

3 January 1852 - The cases or coverings [*chekhly ili nakladki*] introduced for Army Infantry on 8 July 1851 for the **firing nipples** of percussion weapons are to be used in the cavalry [249].

26 January 1852 - The grey **forage caps** of noncombatant lower ranks are ordered to have a band the same color as the collar of combatant lower ranks [250].

16 July 1852 - Cases for the **firing nipples** of percussion weapons are to be fully in accordance with the description confirmed for the infantry, with the only difference being that the small strap of black Russian leather that is attached to the case to hold it to the trigger guard by means of a small slit cut in itself, is not to have any button, and that this small strap itself is to be made 3 vershoks [5 1/4 inches] long instead of 2 1/2 vershoks [4 3/8 inches], since cavalry weapons do not have the sling attachment at the trigger guard to which, in the infantry, the small strap is held [251].

13 August 1853 - When generals and field and company-grade officers of Army Cuirassier regiments are in campaign uniform with **frock coats** without sashes, they are to buckle on the swordbelts over the frock coats [252].

15 November 1853 - The description set forth above for Army Cuirassier regiments regarding a new way to roll soldiers'

greatcoats on saddles, the list of items which the cavalry soldier must have while on campaign and at inspectors' reviews, and the description of various small articles along with directions where they are to be stowed, are all extended with equal force to the regiments of the Guards Cuirassier Division, with the difference that when they are packing the saddle, the folded up skirts or ends of the greatcoat, positioned on the front arch, are to be even with the ends of the pistol cases. Along with this confirmation is given to the following description of a new pattern of **horse furniture** for officers:

Saddle of the previous model, without any changes except that from the top of the front arch there is attached an iron staple for packing the greatcoat, and on the rear arch are fixed three such brackets for packing the valise.

Sweatcloth [potnik] (of two layers of felt)—the previous pattern was lined above and below with black cloth, but with the new pattern the upper part is lined with black calf leather. And on this leather, in the back part of the sweatcloth, on the sides, pockets are made of the same kind of leather, for storing horseshoes. In the center of these pockets are pockets for holding nails. Each pocket is closed with a leather flap, fastened with a leather toggle. The lower part of the sweatcloth is not lined with anything.

Pistol cases [Pistolnyya kobury]—as before, but on the end of each is placed a loop of polished leather that is fastened with the loops (of the same kind of leather) that serve attach the greatcoat to the straps that hold the pistol cases to the saddle. A loop is 1/4 vershok [3/8 inch] wide.

Greatcoat [Shinel'] (not present on the previous horse furniture)—the officer's summer uniform greatcoat is spread out its whole length and folded so that the collar and hem reache the center in six folds, and then the ends are folded to the center so that the folded greatcoat is 1 arshin 6 vershoks [3 feet 2 1/2 inches] long. The folded greatcoat is stowed in a leather case of the same length. This case has circular ends 2 3/4 vershoks [4 7/8 inches] in diameter and an opening along its whole length that is closed with four small straps and iron buckles. Straps with buckles, 1 arshin [28 inches] long, are sewn to the ends of the case. The case with the greatcoat inside is tied in front of the saddle with three straps, of which two are sewn to the case as related above, and pass through a loop positioned at the pistol case, while the third, encircling the case around the middle, passes through an iron bracket fixed to the front arch.

Valise [Chemodan] (did not previously exist)—of the pattern confirmed on 7 April 1853 for light-cavalry officers, of grey-blue cloth, with a case of the same cloth, tied to the rear arch by straps, to appropriately placed iron brackets. The *shabrack [cheprak]* is as before, without any change [253].

29 April 1854 - During wartime, generals and field and company-grade officers are to have campaign **greatcoats**, following the same rules explained for Grenadier regiments [254].

NOTES

(1) HIGHEST Order, 15 December 1825.

(2) Collection of Laws and Directives Relating to the Military Administration, 1826, Book I, pg. 105, § 1, pg. 108, § 6 and pg. 110.

(3) Ibid., Book II, pg. 27

(4) Ibid., Book III, pg. 255.

(5) Ibid., Book IV, pg. 95.

(6) Ibid., 1827, Book I, pg. 3.

(7) Ibid., pg. 153.

(8) Ibid., pg. 205.

(9) Ibid., Book III, pg. 89.

(10) Ibid., Book IV, pg. 257.

(11) Ibid., 1828, Book I, pg. 185.

(12) Ibid., Book II, pp. 131 et seq.

(13) Ibid., 1829, Book II, pg. 221 Ibid., § 12.

(14) Ibid., Book IV, pg. 115, and information from the Commissariat Department of the War Ministry.

(15) Collection of Laws and Directives, 1831, Book II, pg. 39, and information from the Commissariat Department of the War Ministry.

(16) Information from the Commissariat Department of the War Ministry.

(17) Order of the Director of HIS IMPERIAL MAJESTY'S Main Staff, 1 Februray 1832, No. 1.

(18) Collection of Laws and Directives, 1832, Book I, pg. 35.

(19) Ibid., pg. 57.

(20) Ibid., 1832, Book II, pg. 545.

(21) Ibid., 1833, Book I, pg. 419.

(22) Ibid., pg. 435.

(23) Ibid., pg. 463.

(24) Ibid., 1834, Book II, pg. 239.

(25) Ibid., Book III, pg. 465.

(26) Ibid., 1835, Book III, pg. 179.

(27) Ibid., 1836, Book I, pg. 137.

(28) Ibid., Book II, pg. 171.

(29) Ibid., pg. 209.

(30) Ibid., Book IV, pg. 157.

(31) Ibid., 1837, Book I, pg. 353.

(32) Ibid., Book III, pg. 47.

(33) Ibid., Book IV, pg. 325.

(34) Ibid., 1838, Book I, pg. 19.

(35) Ibid., 1839, Book I, pg. 3.

(36) Ibid., pg. 179.

(37) Order of the Minister of War, 16 October 1840, N° 60.

(38) —— —— —— 23 January 1841, N° 8.

(39) —— —— —— 8 April 1843, N° 46.

(40) —— —— —— 8 April 1843, N° 44.

(41) —— —— —— 8 April 1843, N° 47.

(42) —— —— —— 10 May 1843, N° 63.

(43) —— —— —— 2 January 1844, N° 1.

(44) —— —— —— 8 January 1844, N° 3.

(45) —— —— —— 9 May 1844, N°N° 63 and 64.

(46) —— —— —— 20 May 1844, N° 69.

(47) —— —— —— 17 November 1844, N° 138.

(48) —— —— —— 7 December1844, N° 147.

(49) —— —— —— 4 January 1845, N° 1.

(50) —— —— —— 9 August 1845, N° 101.

(51) Correspondence of the Minister of War to HIS IMPERIAL HIGHNESS the Commander-in-Chief of the Guards and Grenadiers Corps, 14 April 1846, N° 3591.

(52) Order of the Minister of War, 26 April 1846, N° 73.

(53) —— —— —— 8 March 1847, N° 46.

(54) —— —— —— 19 May 1847, N° 86.

(55) —— —— —— 29 November 1847, N° 186.

(56) —— —— —— 9 January 1848, N° 8.

(57) —— —— —— 19 April 1849, N° 31.

(58) —— —— —— 14 September 1849, N° 88.

(59) — —   — —   — — 9 and 25 November 1849, N°N° 110 and 117.
(60) — —   — —   — — 24 December 1849, N° 133.
(61) — —   — —   — — 17 January 1851, N° 7.
(62) — —   — —   — — 13 December 1851, N° 133.
(63) — —   — —   — — 20 October 1851, N° 120.
(64) — —   — —   — — 26 January 1852, N° 15.
(65) — —   — —   — — 17 October 1852, N° 110.
(66) — —   — —   — — 3 January 1853, N° 3.
(67) — —   — —   — — 18 February 1854, N° 21.
(68) — —   — —   — — 29 April 1854, N° 53.
(69) — —   — —   — — 14 May 1854, N° 58.
(70) — —   — —   — — 16 June 1854, N° 65.
(71) — —   — —   — — 15 February 1854, N° 93.
(72) — —   — —   — — 13 February 1855, N° 28.
(73) Collection of Laws and Directives Relating to the Military Administration, 1826, Book I, pg. 105, § 1, pg. 108, § 6 and pg. 110.
(74) Ibid., Book II, pg. 27
(75) Ibid., Book III, pg. 255.
(76) Ibid., Book IV, pg. 95.
(77) Ibid., 1827, Book I, pg. 3.
(78) Ibid., pg. 153.
(79) Ibid., Book III, pg. 89.
(80) Ibid., Book IV, pg. 257.
(81) Ibid., 1828, Book I, pg. 185.
(82) Ibid., Book II, pp. 131 et seq.
(83) Ibid., 1829, Book II, pg. 221 Ibid., § 12.
(84) Ibid., Book IV, pg. 115, and information from the Commissariat Department of the War Ministry.
(85) Information from that same Department.
(86) Order of the Director of HIS IMPERIAL MAJESTY'S Main Staff, 1 Februray 1832, No. 1.
(87) Collection of Laws and Directives, 1832, Book I, pg. 57.
(88) Ibid., Book II, pg. 545.
(89) Ibid., 1833, Book I, pg. 419.
(90) Ibid., pg. 435.
(91) Information from the Commissariat Department of the War Ministry.
(92) Ibid., 1833, Book III, pg. 465.
(93) Ibid., 1835, Book III, pg. 179.
(94) Ibid., 1836, Book I, pg. 137.
(95) Ibid., Book II, pg. 171.
(96) Ibid., pg. 209.
(97) Ibid., Book IV, pg. 157.
(98) Ibid., 1837, Book I, pg. 353.
(99) Ibid., Book III, pg. 47.
(100) Ibid., Book IV, pg. 325.
(101) Ibid., 1838, Book I, pg. 19.
(102) Ibid., 1839, Book I, pg. 3.
(103) Ibid., pg. 179.
(104) Order of the Minister of War, 16 October 1840, N° 60.
(105) — —   — —   — — 23 January 1841, N° 8.
(106) — —   — —   — — 8 April 1843, N° 46.
(107) — —   — —   — — 8 April 1843, N° 47.
(108) — —   — —   — — 10 May 1843, N° 63.
(109) — —   — —   — — 2 January 1844, N° 1.
(110) — —   — —   — — 8 January 1844, N° 3.
(111) — —   — —   — — 9 May 1844, N°N° 63 and 64.
(112)   20 May 1844, N° 69.
(113) — —   — —   — — 17 November 1844, N° 138.
(114) — —   — —   — — 7 December1844, N° 147.
(115) — —   — —   — — 4 January 1845, N° 1.
(116) — —   — —   — — 9 August 1845, N° 101.
(117) — —   — —   — — 26 April 1846, N° 73.
(118) — —   — —   — — 8 March 1847, N° 46.
(119) — —   — —   — — 19 May 1847, N° 86.

(120) —— —— —— 29 November 1847, N° 186.
(121) —— —— —— 9 January 1848, N° 8.
(122) —— —— —— 19 April 1849, N° 31.
(123) —— —— —— 14 September 1849, N° 88.
(124) —— —— —— 9 and 25 November 1849, N°N° 110 and 117.
(125) —— —— —— 17 December 1849, N° 129.
(126) —— —— —— 24 December 1849, N° 133.
(127) —— —— —— 17 January 1851, N° 7.
(128) —— —— —— 13 December 1851, N° 134.
(129) —— —— —— 20 October 1851, N° 120.
(130) —— —— —— 26 January 1852, N° 15.
(131) —— —— —— 17 October 1852, N° 110.
(132) —— —— —— 3 January 1853, N° 3.
(133) —— —— —— 18 February 1854, N° 21.
(134) —— —— —— 29 April 1854, N° 53.
(135) —— —— —— 16 July [sic, should be June - M.C.] 1854, N° 65.
(136) —— —— —— 15 February 1854, N° 93.
(137) —— —— —— 13 February 1855, N° 28.
(138) Collection of Laws and Directives, 1829 Book III, pg. 275.
(139) Ibid., 1832, Book II, pg. 545.
(140) Ibid., 1833, Book I, pg. 419.
(141) Ibid., pg. 435.
(142) Ibid., pg. 463.
(143) Ibid., Book III, pg. 437.
(144) Ibid., pg. 465.
(145) Ibid., 1835, Book III, pg. 179.
(146) Ibid., 1836, Book I, pg. 137.
(147) Ibid., Book II, pg. 171.
(148) Ibid., pg. 209.
(149) Ibid., 1837, Book I, pg. 353.
(150) Ibid., Ibid., Book III, pg. 47.
(151) Ibid., Book IV, pg. 325.
(152) Ibid., 1839, Book I, pg. 3.
(153) Ibid., pg. 179.
(154) Order of the Minister of War, 23 January 1841, N° 8.
(155) —— —— —— 8 April 1843, N°N° 46 and 47.
(156) —— —— —— 10 May 1843, N° 63.
(157) Report of the Minister of War to the Commander-in-Chief of the Active Army, 30 August 1843, N° 6918.
(158) —— —— —— 2 January 1844, N° 1.
(159) —— —— —— 9 May 1844, N° 63.
(160) —— —— —— 20 May 1844, N° 69.
(161) —— —— —— 17 November 1844, N° 138.
(162) —— —— —— 4 January 1845, N° 1.
(163) —— —— —— 9 August 1845, N° 101.
(164) Information received from the Life-Guards Finnish Rifle Battalion.
(165) —— —— —— 8 March 1847, N° 46.
(166) —— —— —— 19 May 1847, N° 86.
(167) —— —— —— 29 November 1847, N° 186.
(168) —— —— —— 9 January 1848, N° 8.
(169) —— —— —— 19 April 1849, N° 31.
(170) —— —— —— 14 September 1849, N° 88.
(171) —— —— —— 9 and 25 November 1849, N°N° 110 and 117.
(172) —— —— —— 24 December 1849, N° 129.
(173) —— —— —— 17 December 1851, N° 7.
(174) —— —— —— 13 December 1851, N° 134.
(175) —— —— —— 20 October 1851, N° 120.
(176) —— —— —— 26 January 1852, N° 15.
(177) —— —— —— 28 December 1852, N° 147.
(178) —— —— —— 3 January 1853, N° 3.
(179) —— —— —— 18 February 1854, N° 21.
(180) —— —— —— 29 April 1854, N° 53.

(181) —— —— —— 13 February 1855, Nº 28.
(182) Collection of Laws and Directives, 1826, Book I, pp. 108, 109, and 110.
(183) Ibid., Book II, pg. 121.
(184) Ibid., Book III, pg. 255.
(185) Ibid., 1827, Book I, pg. 3.
(186) Information received from the Commissariat Department of the War Ministry.
(187) Collection of Laws and Directives, 1827, Book IV, pg. 257.
(188) Ibid., 1828, Book I, pg. 141.
(189) Ibid., pg. 211.
(190) Ibid., Book II, pg. 131.
(191) Information received from the Commissariat Department of the War Ministry.
(192) Collection of Laws and Directives, 1829, Book III, pg. 5.
(193) Ibid., pg. 115, and information received from the Commissariat Department of the War Ministry.
(194) Information received from the Commissariat Department of the War Ministry.
(195) Complete Collection of Laws of the Russian Empire, 1830, Nº 3762.
(196) Information received from the Commissariat Department of the War Ministry.
(197) Collection of Laws and Directives, 1830, Book III, pg. 217.
(198) Information received from the Commissariat Department of the War Ministry.
(199) Information received from that same Department.
(200) Collection of Laws and Directives, 1832, Book I, pg. 3.
(201) Information received from the Commissariat Department of the War Ministry.
(202) Collection of Laws and Directives, 1832, Book II, pg. 545.
(203) Information received from the Commissariat Department of the War Ministry.
(204) Information received from that same Department.
(205) Collection of Laws and Directives, 1834, Book II, pg. 237.
(206) Ibid., pg. 239.
(207) Ibid., pg. 245.
(208) Ibid., Book IV, pg. 141.
(209) Information received from the Commissariat Department of the War Ministry.
(210) Collection of Laws and Directives, 1835, Book I, pg. 365.
(211) Ibid., pg. 367.
(212) Ibid., Book II, pp. 79 and 84.
(213) Ibid., 1836, Book I, pg. 137.
(214) Ibid., Book II, pg. 209.
(215) Ibid., 1837, Book III, pg. 47.
(216) Ibid., Book IV, pg. 325.
(217) Ibid., pg. 59.
(218) Ibid., Book IV, pg. 147, and Book I, pg. 339.
(219) Ibid., 1839, Book I, pg. 3.
(220) Order of the Minister of War, 16 October 1840, Nº 71.
(221) —— —— —— 23 January 1841, Nº 8.
(222) Information received from HER MAJESTY'S Cavalier Guards and Life-Guards Horse regiments.
(223) Order of the Minister of War, 31 January 1843, Nº 16.
(224) Information received from the Commissariat Department of the War Ministry.
(225) —— —— —— 8 April 1843, Nº 47.
(226) —— —— —— 10 May 1843, NºNº 63 and 64.
(227) —— —— —— 2 January 1844, Nº 1.
(228) —— —— —— 2 February 1844, Nº 11.
(229) —— —— —— 19 February 1844, Nº 16.
(230) —— —— —— 20 May 1844, Nº 69, pp. 6 and 7.
(231) —— —— —— 21 September 1844, Nº 115.
(232) —— —— —— 27 January 1845, Nº 17.
(233) —— —— —— 29 March 1845, Nº 56.
(234) —— —— —— 15 November 1845, Nº 139.
(235) —— —— —— 19 November 1845, Nº 140.
(236) —— —— —— 2 February 1846, Nº 27.
(237) Correspondence of the Artillery Department of the War Ministry, 13 April 1855, Nº 8347, and HIGHEST confirmed drawings of cuirasses, 17 May 1852.
(238) Order of the Minister of War, 13 September 1846, Nº 160.
(239) —— —— —— 19 May 1847, Nº 86.
(240) —— —— —— 9 January 1848, Nº 8.

(241) — — — — — — 19 January 1848, N° 17.
(242) — — — — — — 25 April 1848, N° 80.
(243) — — — — — — 31 March 1849, N° 29.
(244) — — — — — — 24 December 1849, N° 133.
(245) — — — — — — 5 March 1850, N° 18.
(246) — — — — — — 30 March 1851, N° 36.
(247) — — — — — — 15 April 1851, N° 48.
(248) — — — — — — 25 June 1851, N° 77.
(249) — — — — — — 3 January 1852, N° 2.
(250) — — — — — — 26 January 1852, N° 15.
(251) — — — — — — 16 July 1852, N° 81.
(252) — — — — — — 13 August 1853, N° 61.
(253) — — — — — — 15 November 1853, N° 78.
(254) — — — — — — 29 April 1854, N° 53.

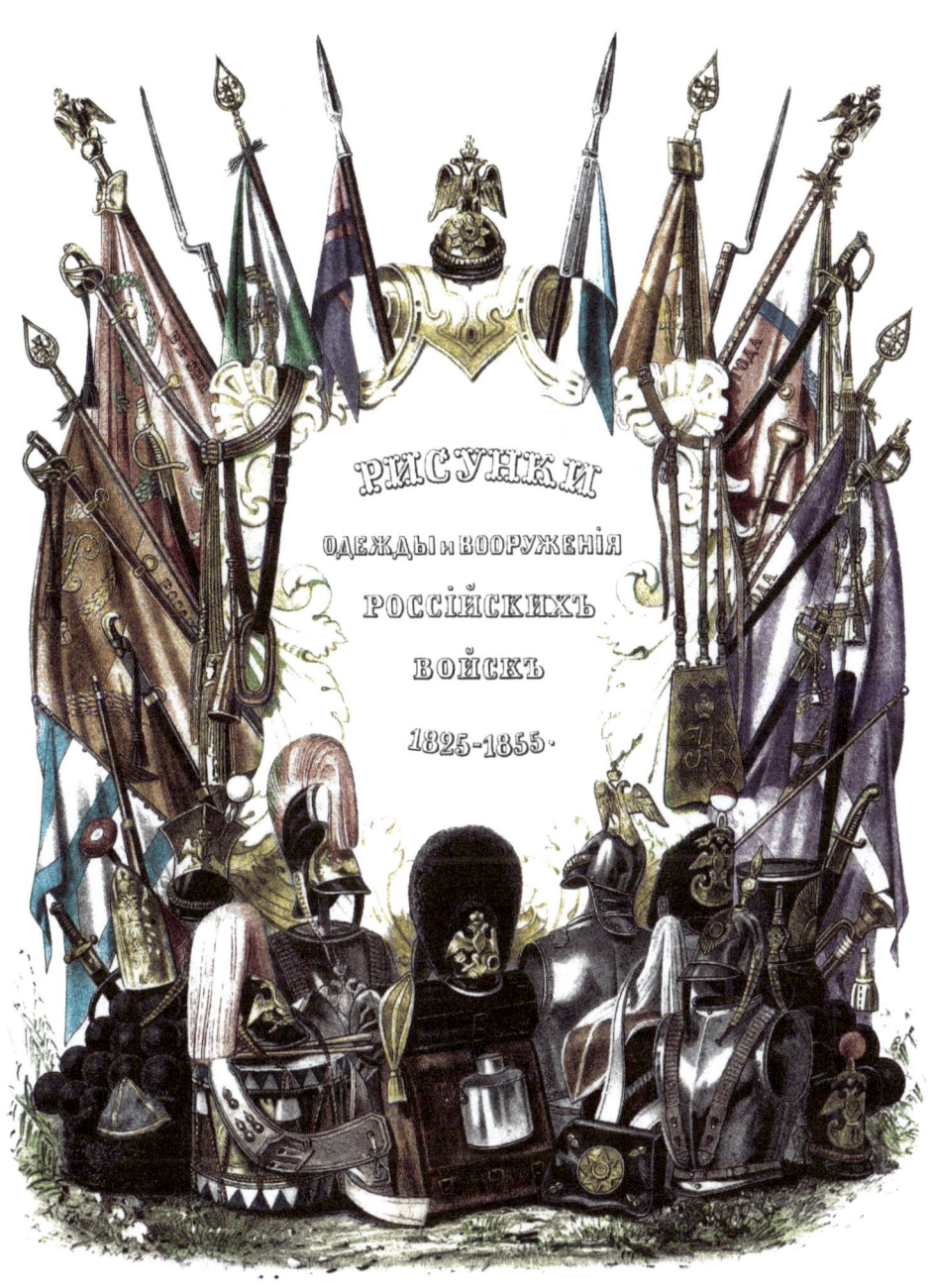

РИСУНКИ

ОДЕЖДЫ и ВООРУЖЕНІЯ

РОССІЙСКИХЪ

ВОЙСКЪ

1825-1855.

PLATES LIST OF ILLUSTRATIONS

642. Private. Life-Guards Preobrazhenskii Regiment. 1846-1855.

643. Distinguished Officer Candidate. Life-Guards Izmailovskii Regiment. 1847-1855.

644. General. Life-Guards Lithuania Regiment. 1848-1855.

645. Private. Life-Guards Grenadier Regiment. 1851-1855.

646. Noncombatant. Life-Guards Semenovskii Regiment. 1852-1855.

647. Officers' Campaign Vice-Shabrack of the Life-Guards Semenovskii Regiment, established 17 October 1852.

648. Field and Company-grade Officers. Life-Guards Preobrazhenskii and Semenovskii Regiments. 1854 and 1855.

649. Privates. Life-Guards Jäger, Finland, and Volhynia Regiments. 1826-1828.

650. Company-Grade Officers. Life-Guards Jäger, Finland, and Volhynia Regiments. 1826-1828.

651. Field-grade Officer. Life-Guards Volhynia Regiment. 1826-1828.

652. Non-commissioned Officer and Company-grade Officer. Life-Guards Finland Regiment. 1827 and 1828.

653. Privates. Life-Guards Jäger, Finland, and Volhynia Regiments. 1828-1831.

654. Company-Grade Officers. Life-Guards Jäger, Finland, and Volhynia Regiments. 1828-1833.

655. Private and Company-grade Officer. Life-Guards Volhynia Regiment. 1831-1833.

656. Private and Company-grade Officer. Life-Guards Volhynia Regiment. 1832 and 1833.

657. Privates. Life-Guards Jäger Regiment. 1833-1843.

658. Hornist and Company-Grade Officer. Life-Guards Finland Regiment. 1833-1843.

659. Drum Major. Life-Guards Jäger Regiment. 1833-1843.

660. Non-commissioned Officers. Life-Guards Finland and Volhynia Regiments. 1834-1843.

661. Non-commissioned Officer, Private, and Musician. Life-Guards Jäger, Finland, and Volhynia Regiments. 1844-1846.

662. Field-grade Officers. Life-Guards Jäger, Finland, and Volhynia Regiments. 1844.

663. Company-grade Officers. Life-Guards Finland and Volhynia Regiments. 1845-1849.

664. Drummer. Life-Guards Jäger Regiment. 1847-1851.

665. Noncombatant. Life-Guards Volhynia Regiment. 1852-1855.

666. Field-grade Officer. Life-Guards Volhynia Regiment. 1852-1855.

667. Drummer, Private, and Non-commissioned Officer. Life-Guards Finnish Rifle Battalion. 1829-1833.

668. Field-grade Officer and Company-grade Officer. Life-Guards Finnish Rifle Battalion. 1829-1833.

669. Shako plate of the Life-Guards Finnish Rifle Battalion, established 16 July 1829.

670. Hornist and Company-grade Officer. Life-Guards Finnish Rifle Battalion. 1833-1843.

671. Private. Life-Guards Finnish Rifle Battalion. 1834-1842.

672. Company-grade Officer. Life-Guards Finnish Rifle Battalion. 1835-1843.

673. Non-commissioned Officer. Life-Guards Finnish Rifle Battalion. 1843 and 1844.

674. Company-grade Officer, Non-commissioned Officer, and Hornist. Life-Guards Finnish Rifle Battalion. 1844.

675. Field-grade Officer. Life-Guards Finnish Rifle Battalion. 1845-1859.

676. Company-grade Officer. Life-Guards Finnish Rifle Battalion. 1845-1849.

677. Rifle of the Life-Guards Finnish Rifle Battalion, produced by HIGHEST Direction in Belgium at the Liège Factory in 1842.

678. Bugler. Life-Guards Finnish Rifle Battalion. 1849-1855.

679. Company-grade Officer. Cavalier Guards Regiment. 1826-1829.

680. Private, Company-grade Officer, and Field-grade Officer. HER MAJESTY'S Leib-Cuirassier Regiment. 1826 and 1827.

681. Non-commissioned Officer, Trumpeter, Private, Field-grade Officer, and Company-grade Officer. Cavalier Guards, Life-Guards Horse, Life-Guards Cuirassier, HER MAJESTY'S Leib-Cuirassier, and Life-Guards Podolia Cuirassier Regiments. 1827 and 1828.

682. Private. Cavalier Guards Regiment. 1828.

683. Company-grade Officer, Non-commissioned Officer, and Private. Cavalier Guards, Life-Guards Horse, and Life-Guards Podolia Cuirassier Regiments. 1828 and 1829.

684. Lower ranks' Cuirass for the Cavalier Guards, Life-Guards Horse, and Life-Guards Podolia Cuirassier Regiments, established in 1828.

685. Field-grade Officer and Non-commissioned Officer. HIS MAJESTY'S Life-Guards Cuirassier Regiment. 1831-1833.

686. Private. HER MAJESTY'S Cavalier Guards Regiment. 1831-1843.

687. Company-grade Officer and Private. HIS MAJESTY'S Life-Guards Cuirassier Regiment. 1833-1843.

688. Officers' Cuirass of HIS MAJESTY'S Life-Guards Cuirassier Regiment, established 27 February 1833.

689. Company-grade Officer and Non-commissioned Officer. The HEIR AND TSESAREVICH'S Leib-Cuirassier Regiment. 1833.

690. Officers' Cuirass of the heir and Tsesarevich's Leib-Cuirassier Regiment, established 18 November 1833.

691. Trumpeter and Company-grade Officer. The heir and Tsesarevich's Leib-Cuirassier Regiment. 1834-1838.

692. Private. HER MAJESTY'S Cavalier Guards Regiment. 1834-1843.

693. Trumpeter. HIS MAJESTY'S Life-Guards Cuirassier Regiment. 1838-1855.

694. Private. Life-Guards Horse Regiment. 1838-1844.

695. Private and Company-grade Officers. HER MAJESTY'S Cavalier Guards and Life-Guards Horse Regiments. 1841-1845.

696. Lower Ranks' Supraveste of the Life-Guards Horse Regiment, established in 1841.

697. General. HIS MAJESTY'S Life-Guards Cuirassier Regiment. 1844-1855.

698. Private. The HEIR AND TSESAREVICH'S Leib-Cuirassier Regiment. 1844.

699. Company-grade Officer and Trumpeter. HER MAJESTY'S Cavalier Guards and Life-Guards Horse Regiments. 1845.

700. Field-grade Officer and Private. HIS MAJESTY'S Life-Guards Cuirassier and the HEIR AND TSESAREVICH'S Leib-Cuirassier Regiments. 1845.

701. Helmet for Guards Cuirassier Regiments, established 27 January 1845.

702. Company-grade Officer and Private. HER MAJESTY'S Cavalier Guards and HIS MAJESTY'S Life-Guards Cuirassier Regiments. 1845.

703. Private. HER MAJESTY'S Cavalier Guards Regiment. Non-commissioned Officer. Life-Guards Horse Regiment. 1846-1851.

704. Company-grade Officers. HIS MAJESTY'S Life-Guards Cuirassier and HIS HIGHNESS THE HEIR AND TSESAREVICH'S Leib-Cuirassier Regiments. 1846-1853.

Monogram of Emperor Alexander I, confirmed by Highest Authority on 15 Dec. 1825 for officers' epaulettes and lower ranks' shoulder straps, for personnel who on the day of HM death were in the First Grenadier companies of the Life-Guards Preobrazhenskii and Semenoskii regiments.

Monogram of Emperor Alexander I, established on 1 March 1827 for officers' and lower ranks' coats.

Privates. Life-Guards Preobrazheskii, Semenovskii, and Izmailovskii Regiments. 1826 and 1827.

609

Non-commissioned Officers. Life-Guards Moscow and Grenadier Regiments. 1826 and 1827.

35

610

Musician. Life-Guards Lithuania Regiment. 1826-1828.

611

Field-grade Officer. Life-Guards Pavlovsk Regiment. 1826 and 1827.

37

Company-grade Officers. Life-Guards Moscow and Grenadier Regiments. 1827 and 1828.

Non-commissioned Officer. Life-Guards Pavlovsk Regiment. 1827-1833.

615

Privates. Life-Guards Preobrazheskii, Semenovskii, and Izmailovskii Regiments. 1828-1833.

40

616

Field-grade Officer. Life-Guards Moscow Regiment. 1828-1843.

Private and Drummer. Life-Guards Grenadier Regiment. 1828-1833.

Non-commissioned Officer and Clerk. Life-Guards Lithuania Regiment. 1828-1833.

Guards Shako Plate, established 24 April 1828.
Shako Plate of the Life-Guards Lithuania Regiment, established 24 April 1828.

Noncombatants. Guards Regiments. From 1828 on.

Field-grade Officer and Hornist. Life-Guards Lithuania Regiment. 1831-1836.

Non-commissioned Officer. Life-Guards Grenadier Regiment. Private. Life-Guards Pavlovsk Regiment. 1831-1833.

Company-grade Officers and Privates. The Emperor of Austria's and the King of Prussia's Grenadier Regiments. 1832 and 1833.

Private and Company-grade Officer. Life-Guards Lithuania Regiment. 1832.

Non-commissioned Officer. Life-Guards Preobrazhenskii Regiment. 1833-1843.

627

Fifer. Life-Guards Semenovskii Regiment. Company-grade Officers. Life-Guards Izmailovskii Regiment. 1833 and 1834.

51

628

Private. The Emperor of Austria's Grenadier Regiment. Drummer. The King of Prussia's Grenadier Regiment. 1834-1843.

52

Non-commissioned Officers. Life-Guards Moscow and Grenadier Regiments. 1834-1843.

630

Company-grade Officer. Life-Guards Pavlovsk Regiment. 1835-1854.

Drum Major. Life-Guards Lithuania Regiment. 1843 and 1844.

632

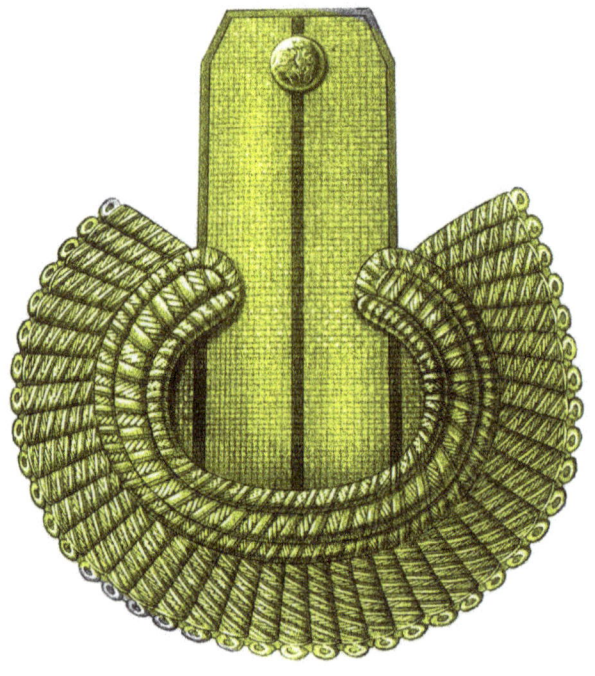

Guards Drum Major's Epaulette, established 8 April 1843.

General. Life-Guards Lithuania Regiment. 1844-1855.

Privates. Life-Guards Preobrazheskii, Semenovskii, and Izmailovskii Regiments. 1844-1846.

Non-commissioned Officer and Fifer. Life-Guards Moscow Regiment. 1844-1855.

Private. Life-Guards Grenadier Regiment. Musician. Life-Guards Lithuania Regiment. 1844-1846

Private. Emperor Francis I's Grenadier Regiment. Durmmer. King Frederick-William III's Grenadier Regiment. 1844-1849.

Company-grade Officers. Life-Guards Preobrazhenskii and Semenovskii Regiments. 1844-1849.

639

Field-grade Officer. Life-Guards Izmailovskii Regiment. 1845-1849.

63

Company-grade Officers. Life-Guards Moscow, Grenadier, and Lithuania Regiments. 1845-1849.

641

Field and Company-grade Officers. Life-Guards Pavlovsk Regiment. 1846-1849.

Private. Life-Guards Preobrazhenskii Regiment. 1846-1855.

643

Distinguished Officer Candidate. Life-Guards Izmailovskii Regiment. 1847-1855.

67

General. Life-Guards Lithuania Regiment. 1848-1855.

645

Private. Life-Guards Grenadier Regiment. 1851-1855.

Noncombatant. Life-Guards Semenovskii Regiment. 1852-1855.

Officers' Campaign Vice-Shabrack of the Life-Guards Semenovskii Regiment, established 17 October 1852.
Shako plate of the Life-Guards Finnish Rifle Battalion, established 16 July 1829.

Field and Company-grade Officers. Life-Guards Preobrazhenskii and Semenovskii Regiments. 1854 and 1855.

649

Privates. Life-Guards Jäger, Finland, and Volhynia Regiments. 1826-1828.

73

Company-Grade Officers. Life-Guards Jäger, Finland, and Volhynia Regiments. 1826-1828.

651

Field-grade Officer. Life-Guards Volhynia Regiment. 1826-1828.

Non-commissioned Officer and Company-grade Officer. Life-Guards Finland Regiment. 1827 and 1828.

653

Privates. Life-Guards Jäger, Finland, and Volhynia Regiments. 1828-1831.

654

Company-Grade Officers. Life-Guards Jäger, Finland, and Volhynia Regiments. 1828-1833.

Private and Company-grade Officer. Life-Guards Volhynia Regiment. 1831-1833.

Private and Company-grade Officer. Life-Guards Volhynia Regiment. 1832 and 1833.

657

Privates. Life-Guards Jäger Regiment. 1833-1843.

81

Hornist and Company-Grade Officer. Life-Guards Finland Regiment. 1833-1843.

659

Drum Major. Life-Guards Jäger Regiment. 1833-1843.

83

Non-commissioned Officers. Life-Guards Finland and Volhynia Regiments. 1834-1843.

661

Non-commissioned Officer, Private, and Musician. Life-Guards Jäger, Finland, and Volhynia Regiments. 1844-1846.

85

Field-grade Officers. Life-Guards Jäger, Finland, and Volhynia Regiments. 1844.

Company-grade Officers. Life-Guards Finland and Volhynia Regiments. 1845-1849.

Drummer. Life-Guards Jäger Regiment. 1847-1851.

665

Noncombatant. Life-Guards Volhynia Regiment. 1852-1855.

89

666

Field-grade Officer. Life-Guards Volhynia Regiment. 1852-1855.

90

667

Drummer, Private, and Non-commissioned Officer. Life-Guards Finnish Rifle Battalion. 1829-1833.

91

668

Field-grade Officer and Company-grade Officer. Life-Guards Finnish Rifle Battalion. 1829-1833.

92

670

Hornist and Company-grade Officer. Life-Guards Finnish Rifle Battalion. 1833-1843

671

Private. Life-Guards Finnish Rifle Battalion. 1834-1842.

94

672

Company-grade Officer. Life-Guards Finnish Rifle Battalion. 1835-1843.

Non-commissioned Officer. Life-Guards Finnish Rifle Battalion. 1843 and 1844.

674

Company-grade Officer, Non-commissioned Officer, and Hornist. Life-Guards Finnish Rifle Battalion. 1844.

97

Field-grade Officer. Life-Guards Finnish Rifle Battalion. 1845-1859.

676

Company-grade Officer. Life-Guards Finnish Rifle Battalion. 1845-1849.

677

Rifle of the Life-Guards Finnish Rifle Battalion, produced by Highest Direction in Belgium at the Liège Factory in 1842.

678

Bugler. Life-Guards Finnish Rifle Battalion. 1849-1855.

101

Company-grade Officer. Cavalier Guards Regiment. 1826-1829.

Private, Company-grade Officer, and Field-grade Officer. HER MAJESTY'S Leib-Cuirassier Regiment. 1826 and 1827.

Non-commissioned Officer, Trumpeter, Private, Field-grade Officer, and Company-grade Officer. Cavalier Guards, Life-Guards Horse, Life-Guards Cuirassier, HER MAJESTY'S Leib-Cuirassier, and Life-Guards Podolia Cuirassier Regiments. 1827 and 1828.

682

Private. Cavalier Guards Regiment. 1828.

683

Company-grade Officer, NCO and Private. Cavalier Guards, Life-Guards Horse, and Life-Guards Podolia Cuirassier Reg.. 1828 and 1829.

106

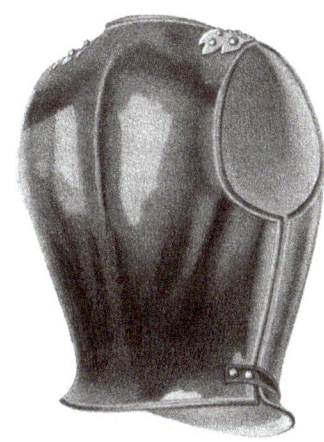

Lower ranks' Cuirass for the Cavalier Guards, Life-Guards Horse, and Life-Guards Podolia Cuirassier Regiments, established in 1828.
Officers' Cuirass of HIS MAJESTY'S Life-Guards Cuirassier Regiment, established 27 February 1833.

685

Field-grade Officer and Non-commissioned Officer. HIS MAJESTY'S Life-Guards Cuirassier Regiment. 1831-1833.

686

Private. HER MAJESTY'S Cavalier Guards Regiment. 1831-1843.

109

Company-grade Officer and Private. HIS MAJESTY'S Life-Guards Cuirassier Regiment. 1833-1843.

689

Company-grade Officer and Non-commissioned Officer. The HEIR AND TSESAREVICH'S Leib-Cuirassier Regiment. 1833.

690-696

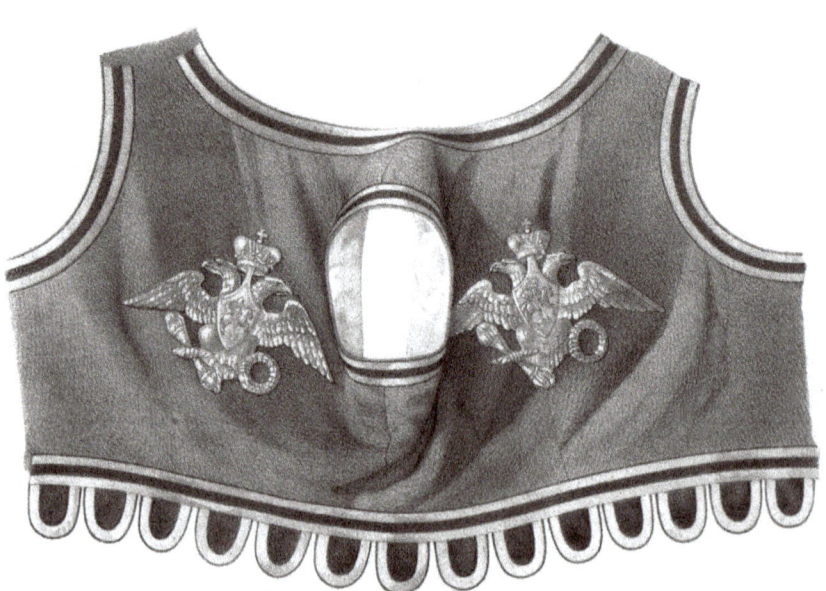

Officers' Cuirass of the HEIR AND TSESAREVICH'S Leib-Cuirassier Regiment, established 18 November 1833.
Lower Ranks' Supraveste of the Life-Guards Horse Regiment, established in 1841.

691

Trumpeter and Company-grade Officer. The HEIR AND TSESAREVICH'S Leib-Cuirassier Regiment. 1834-1838.

113

692

Private. HER MAJESTY'S Cavalier Guards Regiment. 1834-1843.

114

Private. HER MAJESTY'S Cavalier Guards Regiment. 1834-1843.

694

Private. Life-Guards Horse Regiment. 1838-1844.

695

Private and Company-grade Officers. HER MAJESTY'S Cavalier Guards and Life-Guards Horse Regiments. 1841-1845.

697

General. HIS MAJESTY'S Life-Guards Cuirassier Regiment. 1844-1855.

118

Private. The HEIR AND TSESAREVICH'S Leib-Cuirassier Regiment. 1844.

Company-grade Officer and Trumpeter. HER MAJESTY'S Cavalier Guards and Life-Guards Horse Regiments. 1845.

700

Field-grade Officer and Private. HM Life-Guards Cuirassier and the H&T Leib-Cuirassier Regiments. 1845.

121

Company-grade Officer and Private. H.M. Cavalier Guards and HIS MAJESTY'S Life-Guards Cuirassier Regiments. 1845.

703

Private. HER MAJESTY'S Cavalier Guards Regiment. Non-commissioned Officer. Life-Guards Horse Regiment. 1846-1851.

Company-grade Officers. HM Life-Guards Cuirassier and H&J Leib-Cuirassier Regiments. 1846-1853.

701

Helmet for Guards Cuirassier Regiments, established 27 January 1845.

125

SOLDIERS, WEAPONS & UNIFORMS ALREADY PUBLISHED
(SOME TITLES)

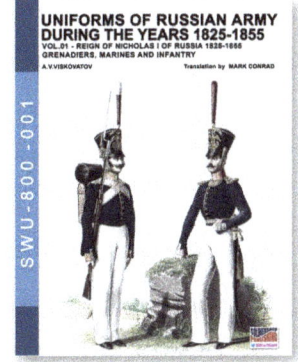

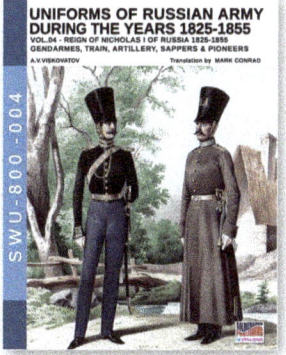

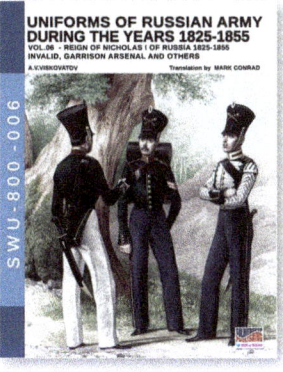

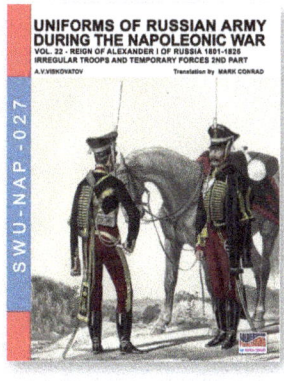

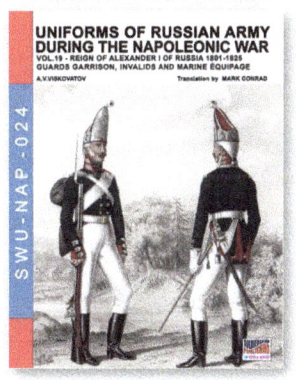
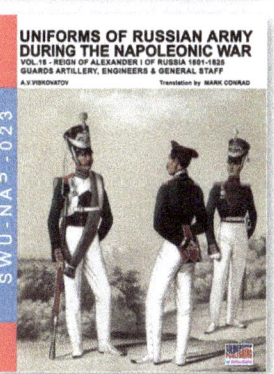

www.ingramcontent.com/pod-product-compliance
Lightning Source LLC
Chambersburg PA
CBHW041143120626
46547CB00020B/3092